The
Random House
Treasury
of
Humorous
Quotations

The Random House Treasury of Humorous Quotations

EDITED BY

William Cole and Louis Phillips

The Random House Treasury of Humorous Quotations

Copyright © 1996 by Louis Phillips and William Cole

All inquiries should be addressed to Reference & Information Publishing,
Random House, Inc., 201 East 50th Street, New York, NY 10022

Published in the United States by Random House, Inc., New York and
simultaneously in Canada by Random House of Canada, Limited, Toronto.

Library of Congress Cataloging-in-Publication Data
The Random House Treasury of Humorous Quotations / edited by Wiliam
   Cole and Louis Phillips.
     p.   cm.
    Includes index.
    ISBN 0-679-77041-0 (hardcover)
    1. Quotations, English. 2. Wit and humor. I. Cole, William,
   1919–   . II. Phillips, Louis.
   PN6084.H8R36 1996
082-dc20   96-27250
                                                  CIP

Typeset and printed in the United States of America

Interior design and page composition by G&H Soho, Hoboken, New Jersey

Visit the Random House Web site at:
http://www.randomhouse.com/

0 9 8 7 6 5 4 3 2 1
First Edition
ISBN 0-679-77041-0

New York Toronto London Sydney Auckland

Time spent laughing is time spent with the gods.

Japanese proverb

Everything I've ever said will be credited to Dorothy Parker.

George S. Kaufman

Introduction

Introductions. Nobody reads them. But our editor said, "introduction?" And what he says goes. This is it.

William Cole
Louis Phillips

Academia

There was an old cannibal whose stomach suffered from so many disorders that he could only digest animals that had no spines. Thus, for years, he subsisted only upon university professors.

Louis Phillips

Who killed James Joyce?
I, said the commentator,
I killed James Joyce
For my graduation.

Patrick Kavanagh

I have lectured on campuses for a quarter of a century, and it is my impression that after taking a course in The Novel, it is an unusual student who would ever want to read a novel again.

Gore Vidal

A friend of mine, contemplating his English department: "There are plenty of vacancies but they're all filled."

Christopher Ricks

Acknowledgments

I feel it is time that I also pay tribute to my four writers, Matthew, Mark, Luke and John.

Bishop Fulton J. Sheen

Acting

The actor who drinks is in a bad way; but the actor who eats is lost.

George Bernard Shaw

An actor's a guy who, if you ain't talking about him, ain't listening.

Marlon Brando

Some of the greatest love affairs I've known involved one actor, unassisted.

Wilson Mizener

Her "Victoria" made me feel that "Albert" had married beneath his station.

Noel Coward, on an actress playing Queen Victoria

I sang every witty couplet with perfect diction and a wealth of implication which sent them winging out in the dark auditorium, where they fell wetly, like pennies into mud.

Noel Coward

The important thing in acting is to be able to laugh and cry. If I have to cry, I think of my sex life. If I have to laugh I think of my sex life.

Glenda Jackson

My dear boy, forget about the motivation. Just say the lines and don't trip over the furniture.

Noel Coward

Joe Leberman says to the method actors: "When I appeared in the crowd scene in *Julius Caesar,* I stood downstage right in extreme profile. I cried only with my right eye. No sense wasting tears that the audience couldn't see."

quoted by Judith Malina in her diaries

Adam

Adam was but human—this explains it all. He did not want the apple for the apple's sake, he wanted it only because it was forbidden. The mistake was not forbidding the serpent; then he would have eaten the serpent.

Mark Twain

Adultery

Sara could commit adultery at one end and weep for her sins at the other, and enjoy both operations at once.

Joyce Cary

I don't say she was above reproach. She was above self-reproach.

Helen Caldwell, on losing her husband to Margaret Bourke-White

A lady temperance candidate concluded her passionate oration, "I would rather commit adultery than take a glass of beer!" Whereupon a clear voice from the audience asked "Who wouldn't?"

No husband can object to his wife's infidelities if she does not blab too much about them. But to hear about the prowess of a Punjabi on Bukit Chandan or a Eurasian on Batu Road is the best of detumescents.

Anthony Burgess

Robert Benchley and I had an office so tiny that an inch smaller and it would have been adultery.

Dorothy Parker

Madame, you must really be more careful. Suppose it had been someone else who found you like this.

*Armand-Emmanuel du Plessis, Duc de Richelieu,
when he discovered his wife with her lover*

Advertising

I have another friend who swears up and down that hordes of people have scratched and sniffed the Carrington and Krystal perfume panels in a recent *People* magazine and thus became hormoneless.

Cynthia Heimel

Batten, Barton, Durstine & Osborne—sounds like a trunk falling down a flight of stairs.

Fred Allen

When the client moans and sighs
make this logo twice the size.
If he still should prove refractory,
show a picture of his factory,
only in the gravest cases
should you show the client's faces.

Anonymous

Advice

I have lived some thirty years on this planet, and I
have yet to hear the first syllable of valuable or
even earnest advice from my seniors.

Henry David Thoreau

What good are vitamins? Eat a lobster, eat a
pound of caviar—live! If you are in love with a
beautiful blonde with an empty face and no brains
at all, don't be afraid. Marry her! Live!

Arthur Rubinstein

Always do right! This will gratify some people and astonish the rest.

Mark Twain

The race is not always to the swift nor the battle to the strong, but that's the way to bet.

Damon Runyon

Ladies and gentlemen,
Here's my advice:
Take off your britches
And slide on the ice.

American folk rhyme

The doghouse is no place to keep a sausage.

American proverb

Do unto the other feller the way he'd like to do unto you an' do it fust.

Edward Noyes Westcott

Never eat at a place called "Mom's." Never play cards with a man named "Doc." And never sleep with anyone whose troubles are worse than your own.

Nelson Algren

A man should swallow a toad every morning if he wishes to be sure of finding nothing still more disgusting before the day is over.

Chamfort

One of the most important things to remember about infant care is: never change diapers in midstream.

Don Marquis

Never moon a werewolf.

Mike Binders

Never trust men with short legs. Brains too near their bottoms.

Noel Coward

1. Avoid fried meats, which angry up the blood.
2. If your stomach disputes you, lie down and pacify it with cool thoughts.
3. Keep the juices flowing by jangling around gently as you move.
4. Go very light on the vices, such as carrying on in society. The social rumble ain't restful.
5. Avoid running at all times.
6. Don't look back. Something might be gaining on you.

Satchel Paige

Put all your eggs in one basket, and—*watch that basket*.

Mark Twain

Never try to teach a pig to sing; it wastes your time and it annoys the pig.

Paul Dickson

Never believe anything until it has been officially denied.

Claud Cockburn

Never put anything on paper, my boy, and never trust a man with a small black moustache.

P. G. Wodehouse

Aerobics

Aerobics has to be the least appealing activity. I don't even know how this word came into being: "aerobics." I guess gym instructors got together and said, "If we're going to charge ten dollars an hour, we can't call it 'jumping up and down.'"

Rita Rudner

Age

I refuse to admit that I am more than fifty-two, even if that does make my sons illegitimate.

Nancy Astor

When I was a boy of fourteen, my father was so ignorant I could hardly stand to have the old man around. But when I got to be twenty-one, I was astonished at how much he had learned in seven years.

Mark Twain

Many a man that couldn't direct ye to the drug store on the corner when he was thirty will get a respectful hearing when age has further impaired his mind.

Peter Finley Dunne

Mes braves, if I only was 70 again!
Georges Clemenceau, on seeing, at age 80, a pretty girl on the Champs Elysees

When a magazine editor telegraphed Cary Grant to inquire about the actor's age, the cable read:
HOW OLD CARY GRANT?
Cary Grant cabled back:
OLD CARY GRANT FINE. HOW YOU?

There are three ages of man: young, middle age, and don't he look good.

Tommy Trinder

The denunciation of the young is a necessary part of the hygiene of older people, and greatly assists the circulation of their blood.

Logan Pearsall Smith

At the end of every year, I add up the time I have spent on the phone on hold and subtract it from my age. I don't count that time as really living. I spend more time on hold each year. By the time I die, I'm going to be quite young.

Rita Rudner

Agents

My agent gets ten percent of everything I get, except my blinding headaches.

Fred Allen

Airlines

He won't fly on the Balinese airline, Garunda,
because he won't fly on any airline where the
pilots believe in reincarnation.

Spalding Gray

America

It was wonderful to find America, but it would
have been more wonderful to miss it.

Mark Twain

To Americans English manners are far more
frightening than none at all.

Randall Jarrell

In the United States there is more space where
nobody is than where anybody is. That is what
makes America what it is.

Gertrude Stein

Americans adore me and will go on adoring me until I say something nice about them.

George Bernard Shaw

What can you say about a society that says God is dead and Elvis is alive?

Irv Kupcinet

England and America are two countries separated by the same language.

George Bernard Shaw

I do not know the American gentleman. God forgive me for putting two such words together.

Charles Dickens

America—a country that has leapt from barbarism to decadence without touching civilization.

John O'Hara

I signed and notarized a document in which I promised not to overthrow the American government by force—a promise I have carefully kept to this day.

Malcolm Bradbury

He held, too, in his enlightened way, that Americans have a perfect right to exist. But he did often find himself wishing Mr. Rhodes had not enabled them to exercise that right in Oxford.

Max Beerbohm

As Oscar Wilde should have said, when bad ideas have nowhere else to go, they emigrate to America and become university courses.

Frederic Raphael

Anatomy

When I was eleven, I thought that women were solid from the neck down.

C. E. M. Joad

No feature of the female form
Should strikingly exceed the norm.
What famous beauty comes to mind
Who boasted an immense behind?

A. P. Herbert

Good cheekbones are the brassiere of old age.

Barbara de Portago

It's more fun contemplating somebody else's navel
than your own.

Arthur Hoppe

Animals

The lion and the lamb may lie down together, but
the lamb won't get much sleep.

Woody Allen

I shoot the Hippopotamus
With bullets made of platinum,
Because if I used leaden ones
His hide is sure to flatten 'em.

Hilaire Belloc

Odd things animals. All dogs look up to you. All cats look down to you. Only a pig looks at you as an equal.

Winston Churchill

Applause

When the people applauded him wildly, he [Phocion] turned to one of his friends and said, "Have I said something foolish?"

Diogenes Laertius

Architecture

A doctor can bury his mistakes, but an architect can only advise his client to plant vines.

Frank Lloyd Wright

In my experience, if you have to keep the lavatory door shut by extending you left leg, it's modern architecture.

Nancy Banks Smith

It looked as though St. Paul's had gone down to the sea and pupped.

Sydney Smith, on Brighton's Royal Pavilion

Think how uncomfortable Hansel and Gretel must have been in the Witch's candy house in damp weather!

C. S. Lewis

Art

I commissioned my portrait bust from Paravinci . . . I doubt he will ever get the stone or finish it; if he does it will be the next best thing to having myself stuffed.

Evelyn Waugh

I can piss the old boy in the snow.

Max Liebermann, German artist, reply to artist who said he couldn't draw Von Hindenberg

He said that Turner's "Slave Ship" floundering about in that fierce conflagration of reds and yellows reminded him of a tortoise-shell cat having a fit in a platter of tomatoes.

Mark Twain

She [the Mona Lisa] looked as if she had just been sick or was about to be.

Noel Coward

The best one can say of most modern creative art is that it is just a little less vulgar than reality.

Oscar Wilde

The artistic temperament is a disease that afflicts amateurs.

G. K. Chesterton

Asthma

Asthma doesn't seem to bother me any more unless
I'm around cigars or dogs. The thing that would
bother me most would be a dog smoking a cigar.

Steve Allen

Astrology

There should be three days a week when no one is
allowed to say: "What's your sign?" Violators would
have their copies of Kahlil Gibran confiscated.

Dick Cavett

Atheism

Not only is there no God, but try getting a plumber
at weekends.

Woody Allen

Auctions

I never knew an auctioneer to lie, unless it was absolutely necessary.

Josh Billings

ಹಿ

Audience

The best audience is intelligent, well-educated and a little drunk.

Alben W. Barkley, U.S. Vice President

Aunts

It is no use telling me that there are bad aunts and good aunts. At the core they are all alike. Sooner or later, out pops the cloven hoof.

P. G. Wodehouse

Austria

Everyone behaves as though they were sick or mad . . . I too am sick and mad. The Germans have too little sense of humor to be really mad . . . they are too pessimistic . . . The Austrians are not too pessimistic so that they can be sick and mad. For that there has to be a certain greatness.

Thomas Bernhard

Autobiography

There are certain professions whose members should be prevented by vigilante bands from ever writing autobiography. . . . I am thinking of actors and actresses, generals, comedians, surgeons, film stars, cricketeers, golfers, footballers, and choreographers.

Benny Green

I was very lucky when I was your age. T.S. Eliot
came to see me. He said, 'American poetry just
needs you, Phil.' He took the bus in Detroit. I was
surprised to see him in a Jewish neighborhood,
but there he was. I said, 'You're Tom Eliot.' He
said, 'Say, Sir, son.' Of course, I'm kidding. It was
a long bus ride from London, from Faber and
Faber.

Philip Levine

Robert Charles Benchley, born Isle of
Wight, September 15, 1807. Shipped as
cabin boy on the Florence J. Marble,
1815. Arrested for bigamy and murder
in Port Said, 1817. Released 1820.
Wrote *Tale of Two Cities*. Married
Princess Anastasia of Portugal 1831.
Children. Prince Rupprecht and several
little girls. Wrote *Uncle Tom's Cabin*,
1850. Editor of Godey's Ladies Book,
1851–1856. Began Les Miserables in
1870. Finished by Victor Hugo, Died
1871. Buried in Westminster Abbey.

Robert Benchley

Ducking for apples—change one letter and it's the story of my life.

Dorothy Parker

Awards

I don't deserve this, but then, I have arthritis and I don't deserve that either.

Jack Benny

Ballet

They were doing the Dying Swan at the ballet, and there was a rumor that some bookmakers had drifted into town from upstate New York and that they had fixed the ballet. There was a lot of money bet on the swan to live.

Woody Allen

Banks

A bank is a place where they lend you an umbrella in fair weather and ask for it back again when it begins to rain.

Robert Frost

Barbecues

Going to a white-run barbecue is, I think, like going to a gentile internist: it might turn out all right, but you haven't made any attempt to take advantage of the percentages.

Calvin Trillin

Bars

Farrell's Bar in Brooklyn had urinals so large they looked like shower stalls for Toulouse-Latrec.

Joe Flaherty

Baseball

The secret of managing is to keep the guys who hate you away from the guys who are undecided.

Casey Stengel

If people don't want to come out to the ball park, nobody's going to stop them.

Yogi Berra

If a horse can't eat it, I don't want to play on it.

Dick Allen, St. Louis outfielder, on artificial turf

Although he is a bad fielder, he is also a very poor hitter.

Ring Lardner

Beach

I can go on a beach and stand perfectly upright . . . for four minutes, with my hands held high above my head, and at the end of that time there will be sand in my pockets, on the back of my neck, around my belt line, and in my pipe.

Robert Benchley

Bees

Bees are not as busy as we think they are. They just can't buzz any slower.

Kin Hubbard

Belgium

Belgium is a country invented by the British to annoy the French.

Charles de Gaulle

Leonard Bernstein

I've always felt that Lenny B. would be all right if one could kidnap him and hold him prisoner, far from everything that could remind him of the concept of being successful.

Paul Bowles

Biography

Breaking the ice in the pitcher seems to be a feature of the early lives of all great men.

Robert Benchley

Birmingham, England

One has no great hopes of Birmingham, I always say there is something direful in the sound.

Jane Austen

Birth

Having a baby is like taking your lower lip and forcing it over your head.

Carol Burnett

The way to be born was alone, with a twenty-thousand-pound note pinned to your diaper.

Samuel Butler

Book Reviewing

Your manuscript is both good and original; but the parts that are good are not original, and the parts that are original are not good.

Samuel Johnson

I never read a book before reviewing it; it prejudices one so.

Sydney Smith

Booksellers

To talk to ninety-five percent of the booksellers about books is like a nightmare in which you found yourself discussing meat with a butcher who held Shaw's views of meat, meat-eating and meat selling.

Leonard Woolf

The principle of procrastinated rape is said to be the ruling one in all the great bestsellers.

V.S. Pritchett

If you want to get rich from writing, write the sort of thing that's read by persons who move their lips when they're reading to themselves.

Don Marquis

Boredom

I'm so bored in the town where I live, I know all the vending machines by name.

David Lewis

So little time, so little to do.

Oscar Levant

Somebody's boring me—I think it's me.

Dylan Thomas

Early to rise and early to bed makes a male healthy and wealthy and dead.

James Thurber

Boys

Boys do not grow up gradually. They move forward in spurts like the hands of clocks in railway stations.

Cyril Connolly

Breakfast

I went into a place to eat. It said "Breakfast Anytime," so I ordered French toast during the Renaissance.

Steven Wright

Bridge

Bridge, because of its tendency to encourage pro-
longed smoking and its deadly immobility, is probably the most dangerous game played in England
now.

Anonymous

Bridgeport, Connecticut

New Haven minus Yale equals Bridgeport.

Harold Bloom

Broadway

What a glorious garden of wonders the lights of Broadway would be to anyone lucky enough to be unable to read.

G. K. Chesterton

Business

There is a joke told in London business circles that when a company is about to fall apart it first moves into a building with an atrium.

Stephen Schiff

Canada

In a Doris Day soi-disant sex comedy, Doris's niceness is signalled by the lengths to which she'll go to avoid sex. Today, alas, that would mark her out as some sort of Christian fundamentalist whacko for the Southern virgin cult True Love Waits. So, in *French Kiss*, Meg Ryan's niceness is signalled by the lengths to which she'll go to become Canadian.

Mark Steyn

For some reason, a glaze passes over people's faces when you say Canada.

Sondra Gotlieb, Ambassador's wife

Capitalism

Under capitalism man exploits man; under socialism the reverse is true.

Polish proverb

Capital Punishment

The long and distressing controversy over capital punishment is very unfair to anyone meditating murder.

Geoffrey Fisher

I went out to Charing Cross to see Major-General Harrison drawn and quartered—which was done there—he looking as cheerful as any man could do in that condition.

Samuel Pepys

Catholics

Confessions on Saturday, Absolution on Sunday. At it again on Monday.

H. G. Wells

Cats

Instructions for getting rid of an unwanted cat in a city apartment: Put cat in elevator, press 1.

Sally Fly

Cats are smarter than dogs. You can't get eight cats to pull a sled through snow.

Jeff Valdez

If a man could be crossed with a cat, it would improve man, but it would deteriorate the cat.

Mark Twain

Character

He had a Way of turning Things over with his Fork, as if to say, "Well, I don't know about this."

George Ade

He reminds me of the man who murdered both his parents, and then, when sentence was about to be pronounced pleaded for mercy on the grounds that he was an orphan.

Abraham Lincoln

Chemistry

I bought some powdered water, but I didn't know what to add.

Steven Wright

Childhood

The highlight of my childhood was making my brother laugh so hard that food came out of his nose.

Garrison Keillor

Child Rearing

The reason for the success of *Clan of the Cave Bear* is that it's about a Cro-Magnon child being raised by a family of Neanderthals—a position almost all of us have been in.

Lawrence Block

Children

In general my children refused to eat anything that hadn't danced on TV.

Erma Bombeck

Insanity is hereditary; you get it from your children.

Sam Levenson

Parenthood: that state of being better chaperoned than you were before marriage.

Marcelene Cox

To think those flawless sounds [from the Cathedral] should be produced by twenty vicious, spotty little boys.

W. Douglas Home

There's not a man in America who at one time or another hasn't had a secret desire to boot a child in the ass.

W. C. Fields

I read one psychologist's theory that said, "Never strike a child in anger." When could I strike him? When he is kissing me on my birthday?

Erma Bombeck

Th' worst sensation I know of is gittin' up in th' night an' steppin' on a toy train o' cars.

Kin Hubbard

Before I got married I had six theories about bringing up children; now I have six children, and no theories.

John Wilmot, Earl of Rochester

Children's Books

You know how it is in the kids' book world: It's just bunny eat bunny.

Anonymous

Christmas

In early January friendly Christmas cards continue to arrive, struggling gamely home like the last few stragglers on a London Marathon.

Arthur Marshall

Christmas is already causing considerable anxiety. I often think of running away to a country hotel for a few days in the hope that it might be vaguely Dickensian but the reality would be rooms full of yuppies wearing silly paper hats.

Jeffrey Bernard

I never believed in Santa Claus because I knew no white dude would come into my neighborhood after dark.

Dick Gregory

The way in which Father Christmas's sack is over-loaded clearly contravenes all the safety regulations for the carriage of goods by air.

Lord Mancroft

Cleveland, Ohio

You gotta live somewhere.

Jimmy Brogan, suggesting a motto for Cleveland, Ohio

Colds

A bad cold wouldn't be so annoying if it weren't for the advice of our friends.

Kin Hubbard

College

I find that the three major administrative problems on a campus are sex for the students, athletics for the alumni and parking for the faculty.

Clark Kerr, President, University of California

Communism

The Un-American Activities Committee will nail anyone who even scratched his ass during the National Anthem.

Humphrey Bogart

Conduct

I should never be allowed out in private.

Randolph Churchill, letter of apology to a hostess whose dinner party he had drunkenly ruined

Confusion

In Philadelphia I met a large and interesting family named Scrapple. They served me a rather delicious native food, too—something, I believe, called biddle.

Edward VII

Pyke Johnson Jr. reports this "overheard" in his column in the Greenwich, CT, *Time*. A hostess at a dinner party was asked what cheese she was serving. She looked at the package and said, "It's Italian, Ringondeli."

Congress

I believe if we introduced the Lord's Prayer here, Senators would propose a large number of amendments to it.

Sen. Henry Wilson

Conscience

Conscience is the inner voice that warns us somebody may be looking.

H. L. Mencken

Conservatives

Conservative ideal of freedom and progress: everyone to have an unfettered opportunity of remain-
ing exactly where they are.

Geoffrey Madan

Contraception

I'm Catholic. My mother and I were unpacking
and she found my diaphragm. I had to tell her it
was a bathing cap for my cat.

Lizz Winstead

I want to tell you a terrific story about oral contraception. I asked this girl to sleep with me and she said "No."

Woody Allen

Contracts

A verbal contract isn't worth the paper it's written on.

Samuel Goldwyn

Cooking

Her cooking suggested she had attended the Cordon noir.

Leo Rosten

Courage

I should have the courage of my lack of convictions.

Tom Stoppard

Courtrooms

The penalty for laughing in the courtroom is six months in jail. If it were not for this penalty, the jury would never hear the evidence.

H. L. Mencken

Credit Managers

Possibly the first sign that you are becoming a fiscal leper will be the word 'frankly' cropping up in your business correspondence. 'Frankly' is a word that all credit managers know and like; as they use it, it is pregnant with connotations. It means 'one of the few rewards of this lousy little clerk's job is being rude to people to whom I am no longer under any obligation to be polite, so here goes.'

Russell Maloney

Crime

If you shoot a mime, should you use a silencer?

Steven Wright

I wanted to be an arch-criminal as a child, before I discovered I was too short.

Steven Allen

It is no secret that organized crime in America takes in over forty billion dollars a year. This is quite a profitable sum, especially when one considers that the Mafia spends very little for office supplies.

Woody Allen

A criminal is a person with predatory instincts who has not sufficient capital to form a corporation.

Howard Scott

You're not going to believe this. I saw a murder, I got there five minutes after it happened. Apparently, from what I saw, the body fell into a chalk line exactly the same shape.

Howie Mandel

Critics/Criticism

Who does that Frog think he is to come over here and try to tell us how to play? We don't go over there and tell them how to jump on a grape.

Eddie Condon, reaction to French jazz critic Hughes Panassié

I had a dream the other day about music critics. They were small and rodent-like with padlocked ears, as if they had stepped out of a painting by Goya.

Igor Stravinsky

Critics can't even make music by rubbing their back legs together.

Mel Brooks

Your couplet would have been excellent if it weren't so long.

Nicolas Chamfort

It's more than magnificent. It's mediocre.

Samuel Goldwyn

You managed to play the first act of my little comedy tonight with all the Chinese flair and light-hearted brilliance of Lady Macbeth.

Noel Coward, to Marti Stevens, on her performance in
Blithe Spirit, 1964

Has anybody ever seen a dramatic critic in the daytime? Of course not. They come out after dark, up to no good.

P.G. Wodehouse

It had only one fault. It was kind of lousy.

James Thurber

It was one of those plays in which the actors, unfortunately, enunciated very clearly.

Robert Benchley

Dance

Nureyev and a drowsily sexy ballerina engaged in a long attempt to pull each other's tights off without using fingers.

Clive James

Disco dancing is really music for people who hate dancing . . . There is no syncopation, just the steady thump of a giant moron knocking in an endless nail.

Clive James

The tights on the male dancers were so tight you could see what religion they are.

Robin Williams, on The David Letterman Show

Peter Townsend once had, as in some frightful nightmare, to teach Queen Mary how to dance the Hokey Pokey.

Arthur Marshall

He makes you feel more danced against than with.

Sally Poplin

54

Dating

How many of you ever started dating someone because you were too lazy to commit suicide?

Judy Tenuta

When I'm dating I look at a guy and wonder, "Is this the man I want my children to spend their weekends with?"

Rita Rudner

I'm always attracted to the wrong kind of guy—like the Pope.

Carol Leifer

Death

There is nothing like a morning funeral for sharpening the appetite for lunch.

Arthur Marshall

It is rumored that Piso is dead. It is a great loss. He was a good man and deserved a longer life. He was talented and reliable, resolute and courageous, faithful and generous. Provided of course that he really is dead.

La Bruyère

The chief problem about death, incidentally, is the fear that there may be no afterlife—a depressing thought, particularly for those who have bothered to shave. Also there is the fear that there is an afterlife but no one will know where it's being held.

Woody Allen

Dedications

Dedicated gratefully to the warden and fellows of St. Antony's College, Oxford. Except one.

James Morris

To my loving wife, but for those constant interruptions, this book would have been finished six months earlier.

Franklin P. Adams

Democracy

I'm all in favor of the democratic principle that one idiot is as good as one genius, but I draw the line when someone takes the next step and concludes that two idiots are better than one genius.

Leo Szilard

Description

With those delicate features of his he would have made a pretty woman, and he probably never has.

Jascha Heifetz

Dice

Dice are small polka-dotted cubes of ivory, constructed like a lawyer to lie on any side.

Ambrose Bierce

ॐ

Diplomacy

Diplomacy is the art of saying "Nice doggie" till you can find a rock.

Wynn Catlin

You should never offend either a publicist or a trombone player. If you get on the wrong side of either of them, you're fucked.

Rosaleen Linehan

A diplomat's life is made up of three ingredients: protocol, Geritol and alcohol.

Adlai E. Stevenson

Disasters

I rang for ice, but *this* is ridiculous!

Madeline Talmadge Astor, as she was helped over the rail of the Titanic

Divorce

It's relaxing to go out with my ex-wife because she already knows I'm an idiot.

Warren Thomas

Dogs

I have always thought of a dog lover as a dog that was in love with another dog.

James Thurber

The next-door neighbors had a pro-German police dog that . . . acts as a body guard for the lady of the house and one day we was over there and the host says to slap his Mrs. on the arm and see what happened so I slapped her on the arm and I can still show you what happened.

Ring Lardner

The doggie in front has suddenly gone blind, and the other one has very kindly offered to push him all the way to St. Dunstan's.

Noel Coward, explaining to a 5-year-old
what two dogs were doing

Muggs was always sorry, Mother said, when he bit someone, but we could never understand how she figured this out. He didn't act sorry.

James Thurber

A dog teaches a boy fidelity, perseverance, and to turn around three times before lying down.

Robert Benchley

They say the dog is man's best friend. I don't believe that. How many of your friends have you neutered?

Larry Reeb

Dogs, like horses, are quadrupeds. That is to say, they have four rupeds, one at each corner, on which they walk.

Frank Muir

When my dog Montmorency meets a cat, the whole street knows about it; and there is enough bad language wasted in ten seconds to last an ordinary respectable man all his life.

Jerome K. Jerome

My name was in large type, right across the bottom of the bill declaring that I was "The Popular Comedian." The first bill I saw displayed on a hoarding was close to the ground, and the local dogs had already given their opinion of me.

Arthur Askey

Dachshunds are ideal dogs for small children, as they are already stretched and pulled to such a length that the child cannot do much harm one way or another.

Robert Benchley

If you want to cure your dog's bad breath, just pour a little Lavoris in the toilet.

Jay Leno

The ideal age for a boy to own a dog is between forty-five and fifty. By this time the boy ought to have attained full growth and, provided he is ever going to, ought to know more or less what he wants to make of himself in life.

Robert Benchley

Newfoundland dogs are good to save children from drowning, but you must have a pond of water handy and a child, or else there will be no profit in boarding a Newfoundland.

Josh Billings

They say a reasonable amount 'o fleas is good fer a dog—keeps him from broodin' over *bein'* a dog, mebbe.

Edward Noyes Westcott

I have never stretched myself on a beach for an afternoon's nap that a dog, fresh from a swim, did not take up a position just to the left of my tightly closed eyes, and shake himself.

Robert Benchley

If you see a dog scampering across the grass in Germany, you may know for certain that it is the dog of some unholy foreigner.

Jerome K. Jerome

. . . our late lamented English setter, who was spoilt, goofy, terrifyingly tenacious and possessed of a totally unbridled sex drive. If he got on the trail of a bitch, he would charge across three main roads, race twenty miles until he caught up with her and then mount her from the wrong end.

Jilly Cooper

Irish setters are so dumb they get lost on the end of their leash.

Dr. Michael Fox

Wanted: A dog that neither barks nor bites, eats broken glass and shits diamonds.

Goethe

Dress

Join a Highland regiment, me boy. The kilt is an unrivalled garment for fornication and diarrhoea.

John Masters

Drink

Why don't you slip out of those wet clothes and into a dry martini?

> *Robert Benchley, (sometimes ascribed to*
> *Alexander Woollcott)*

There's nothing worse than an introspective drunk.

> *Tom Sharpe*

An alcoholic is someone you don't like who drinks as much as you do.

> *Dylan Thomas*

A sudden violent jolt of it [moonshine whiskey] has been known to stop the victim's watch, snap his suspenders and crack his glass eye right across.

> *Irvin S. Cobb*

Mona Lisa cocktail—two of them and you can't get that silly grin off your face.

> *Anonymous*

Alcohol is like love: the first kiss is magic, the second is intimate, the third is routine. After that you just take the girl's clothes off.

Raymond Chandler

A good general rule [with wine] is to state that the bouquet is better than the taste, and vice versa.

Stephen Potter

A dusty thudding in his head made the scene before him beat like a pulse. His mouth had been used as a latrine by some small creature of the night and then as its mausoleum.

Kingsley Amis, on a hangover

I distrust camels, and anyone else who can go a week without a drink.

Joe E. Lewis

Each move was as difficult as getting a combative drunken man out of the nightclub in which he fancies he has been insulted.

James Thurber

Doubt

I respect faith, but doubt is what gets you an education.

Wilson Mizener

Dutch

Like the Germans, the Dutch fall into two quite distinct physical types: the small, corpulent, red-faced Edams, and the thinner, paler, large Goudas.

Alan Coren

Eating

You don't have to take your eyes off the book to pick about among it, it's all the same.

Philip Larkin, on his reason for liking spaghetti

Economics

No real English gentleman, in his secret soul, was every sorry for the death of a political economist.

Walter Bagehot

An economist is a man who wears a watch chain with a Phi Beta Kappa key at one end and no watch at the other.

Harry S. Truman

Education

One of the first things a boy learns when he gets a drum set for Christmas is that he isn't likely to ever get another one.

Anonymous

But, good gracious, you've got to educate him first. You can't expect a boy to be vicious till he's been to a good school.

Saki

Stand firm in your refusal to remain conscious during algebra. In real life, I assure you, there is no such thing as algebra.

Fran Lebowitz

Eggs

The English wit, F. E. Smith, was at a dinner party where the main course was tongue. His dinner companion, a dignified lady, said "How disgusting to eat something that had once been in an animal's mouth!"

"Have an egg," Smith rejoined.

Ego

The reason they're giving for the divorce is that Donald Trump has been having a long term affair with himself.

Arsenio Hall

The affair between Margot Asquith and Margot Asquith will live as one of the prettiest love stories in all literature.

Dorothy Parker

I have a certain hesitation in starting my biography too soon for fear of something important having not yet happened. Suppose I should end my days President of Mexico; the biography would seem incomplete if it did not mention this fact.

Bertrand Russell

Embarrassment

It was embarrassing; I felt like the figure skater
who'd forgotten her knickers.

Hugh Leonard

England/the English

In England, if you are a Duchess, you don't need
to be well-dressed—it would be thought quite
eccentric.

Nancy Mitford

By midday the heat is so unbearable that the
streets are empty but for thousands of Englishmen taking mad dogs for walks.

Spike Milligan

The way to endure summer in England is to have
it framed and glazed in a comfortable room.

Horace Walpole

You should study the Peerage. It is the one book a man about town should know thoroughly, and it is the best thing in fiction the English have ever done.

Oscar Wilde

The monarchy is so extraordinary *useful*. When Britain wins a battle she shouts, 'God save the Queen." When she loses, she votes down the prime minister.

Winston Churchill

If you want to eat well in England, eat three breakfasts.

W. Somerset Maugham

Christopher Martin-Jenkins and Neil Durden-Smith were standing there next to the bar skittles, playing with each other's hyphens.

Peter Tinniswood

The English think incompetence is the same thing as sincerity.

Quentin Crisp

72

Iran is an awful country. Women get stoned when they commit adultery. Unlike Britain, where women commit adultery when they get stoned.

Antony Jay & Jonathan Lynn

We have trained our waiters in the dining room not to give us iced water and our chauffeur not to ask us questions. This is here the exact opposite of the English custom by which the upper classes are expected to ask personal questions of the lower.

Evelyn Waugh

The most dangerous thing in the world is to make a friend of an Englishman, because he'll come sleep in your closet rather than spend ten shillings on a hotel.

Truman Capote

One has often wondered whether upon the whole earth there is anything so unintelligent, so unapt to perceive how the world is really going, as an ordinary young Englishman of our upper classes.

Matthew Arnold

The good manners of educated Englishmen . . .
Such leaping to feet, such opening of doors, such
lightning flourishes with matches and cigarettes—
it's all so heroic. I never quite get over the feeling
that someone has just said, "To the lifeboats!"

Margaret Halsey

English language

When we Americans are done with the English
language, it will look as if it had been run over by
a musical comedy.

Finley Peter Dunne

Envy

Whenever a friend succeeds, a little something in
me dies.

Gore Vidal

74

Epigrams

An epigram is a half-truth so stated as to irritate
the person who believes the other half.

Shailer Mathews

If with the literate, I am
Impelled to try an epigram,
I never seek to take the credit;
We all assume that Oscar said it.

Dorothy Parker, "Oscar Wilde"

Eternity

Eternity's a terrible thought. I mean, where's it
going to end?

Tom Stoppard

Etiquette

George Moore, when asked for advice on how to treat two women on either side of him at a formal dinner party: Don't touch their knees, women have an instinctive knowledge whether a man who touches her knee is caressing her or only wiping his greasy fingers on her stocking.

This brings up the interesting question of introducing two people to each other, neither of whose names you can remember. This is generally done by saying very quickly to one of the parties. "Of course you know Miss Unkunkunk." Say the last 'unk' very quickly, so that it sounds like any name from Ab to Zinc. You might even sneeze violently.

Donald Ogden Stewart

Excess

Moderation is a fatal thing. Nothing succeeds like excess.

Oscar Wilde

Excuses

VERY SORRY CAN'T COME. LIE FOLLOWS
BY POST.

Lord Charles Beresford, telegram to Prince of Wales
declining dinner invitation on short notice

Experience

Experience is a hard teacher because she gives the
test first, the lesson afterward.

Vernon Law

Faith

God is love, but get it in writing.

Gypsy Rose Lee

If there was no faith there would be no living in this world. We couldn't even eat hash with any safety.

Josh Billings

Fame

The best fame is a writer's fame. It's enough to get a table at a good restaurant, but not enough to get you interrupted when you eat.

Fran Lebowitz

Family

They were a tense and peculiar family, the Oedipuses, weren't they?

Max Beerbohm

Unlike the male codfish which, suddenly finding itself the parent of three million five hundred thousand little codfish, cheerfully resolves to love them all, the British aristocracy is apt to look with a somewhat jaundiced eye on its younger sons.

P. G. Wodehouse

Fashion

Scientific studies have shown that if a generation has no passion for shoes, it is dead from the neck down.

Cynthia Heimel

There is invariably something queer about women who wear ankle socks.

Alan Bennett

Fate

There is one woman whom fate has destined for each of us. If we miss her we are saved.

Anonymous

Faults

When you have committed a fault, be pert and insolent, and behave as if you were the injured person.

Jonathan Swift

Faux Pas

The only time I ever heard a bigger laugh in classroom was when a master announced, "I want to see John P. in my study immediately after lunch."

John Pertwee

FBI

The FBI is filled with Fordham graduates keeping tabs on Harvard men in the State Department.

Daniel P. Moynihan

Feminism

I myself have never been able to find out precisely what feminism is: I only know that people call me a feminist whenever I express sentiments that differentiate me from a doormat.

Rebecca West

Filmmaking

Shoot a few scenes out of focus. I want to win the foreign film award.

Billy Wilder, to his cameraman

Never shoot a film in Belgrade, Yugoslavia! The whole town is illuminated by a 20 watt night light and there's nothing to do. You can't even go for a drive. Tito is always using the car.

Mel Brooks

Fish

All fishes, of course, lack the mimetic or facial muscles so characteristic of the mammals, and are therefore unable to express their emotions above the neck. The emotions of most fishes would be difficult to express, anyway.

Will Cuppy

Flattery

Baloney is the unvarnished lie laid on so thick you hate it. Blarney is flattery laid on so thin you love it.

Bishop Fulton J. Sheen

I hate careless flattery, the kind that exhausts you in your effort to believe it.

Wilson Mizener

Flowers

All flowers are flirtatious—particularly if they carry hyphenated names. The more hyphens in the name, the flirtier the flower. The one-hyphen flowers—black-eyed Susan; lady-smock; musk-rose—may give you only a shy glance and then drop their eyes; the two-hyphen flowers—forget-me-not; flower-de-luce—keep glancing. Flowers with three or more hyphens flirt all over the garden and continue even when they are cut and arranged in vases. John-go-to-bed-at-noon does not go there simply to sleep.

Willard R. Espy

Flying

I know that experts say you're more likely to get hurt crossing the street than you are flying (these, of course, would be street-crossing experts), but that doesn't make me any less frightened of flying. If anything, it makes me more afraid of crossing the street.

Ellen DeGeneres

Food

Birds in their little nests agree
with Chinamen, but not with me.

Hilaire Belloc

"Turbot, Sir," the waiter said, placing before me two wishbones, two eyeballs, and a bit of black mackintosh.

Thomas Earle Welby

He was a bold man that first ate an oyster.

Jonathan Swift

That hot Chinese cooking can really Szechuan
your ass.

Wilfrid Sheed

What a friend we have in cheeses!
For no food more subtly pleases,
Nor plays so vast a gastronomic part;
Cheese imported—not domestic—
For we all get indigestic
From the pasteurizer's Kraft and sodden art.

William Cole

This piece of cod passes all understanding.

Sir Edward Lutyens

Cheese—milk's leap forward to immortality.

Clifton Fadiman

France/the French

The French language is a pianoforte without a
pedal.

Andre Gide

A bad liver is to a Frenchman what a nervous breakdown is to an American. Everyone has had one and everyone wants to talk about it.

Art Buchwald

Boulliabaisse is only good because cooked by the French, who, if they cared to try, could produce an excellent and nutritious substitute out of cigar stumps and empty matchboxes.

Norman Douglas

In France you are always in a witness-box . . . You must sharpen your wits if you want a favourable verdict.

Nancy Mitford

France is a country where the money falls apart in your hands and you can't tear the toilet paper.

Billy Wilder

The French are going the Americans one better with their Michelin bomb; it destroys only restaurants under four stars.

Robin Williams

My French stinks. It seems that when I asked
somebody for a light I asked them to set me on fire.
Jeffery Bernard

The French are tremendous snobs, despite that
rather showy and ostentatious Revolution.
Arthur Marshall

The French, for instance, cannot get the hang of
standing in line. They try and try, but it's beyond
them. Whenever you go to Paris, you see orderly
lines waiting at bus stops, but as soon as the bus
pulls up, the line instantly disintegrates into
something like a fire drill at a lunatic asylum and
everyone scrambles to be the first aboard.
Bill Bryson

Yet, who can help loving the land that has taught us
six hundred and eighty-five ways to dress an egg?
Thomas Moore

How can you be expected to govern a country that
has two hundred and forty-six kinds of cheese?
Charles de Gaulle (attrib.)

They are short, blue-vested people who carry their own onions when cycling abroad, and have a yard which is 3.37 inches longer than other people's.

Alan Coren

It is unthinkable for a Frenchman to arrive at middle age without having syphilis and the Cross of the Legion of Honor.

Andre Gid

My attitude to France was, I suppose, inherited from my father, who always felt perfectly at home there because he never attempted to talk or make friends with the natives.

Robert Morley

Friends

Friends: people who borrow my books and set wet glasses on them.

Edward Arlington Robinson

Funerals

In the city a funeral is just an interpretation of traffic; in the country it is a form of entertainment.

George Ade

Fury

There is no fury like an ex-wife searching for a new lover.

Cyril Connolly

Gardening

Perennials are the ones that grow like weeds, biennials are the ones that die this year instead of next and hardy annuals are the ones that never come up at all.

Katharine Whitehorn

Gentlemen

A gentleman is a man who can play the trumpet but doesn't.

Lord Chesterfield

A gentleman is a patient wolf.

Henrietta Tiarks

A gentleman need not know Latin, but he should at least have forgotten it.

Brander Matthews

Germans/German Language

A German plants seven rose-trees on the north side and seven on the south, and if they do not grow up all the same size and shape it worries him so that he cannot sleep.

Jerome K. Jerome

German is the most extravagantly ugly language
. . . like someone using a sick-bag on a 747.

William Rushton

It should have been written into the armistice
treaty that the Germans would be required to lay
down their accordions along with their arms.

Bill Bryson

German is a language which was developed solely
to afford the speaker the opportunity to spit at
strangers under the guise of polite conversation.

National Lampoon

God

God, whom you doubtless remember as that
quaint old subordinate to General Douglas
MacArthur.

S. J. Perelman

Santa Claus is preferable to God in every way but one: There is no such thing as Santa Claus.

P. J. O'Rourke

Surely there must be a better gift God could have given us than life

Michael O'Donoghue

Why is it when we talk to God, we're said to be praying—but when God talks to us, we're schizophrenic?

Lily Tomlin

Golf

When I am reincarnated I'm coming back as a golf ball—the men may knock them about and swear at them but they are faithful to them, and they will chase them farther than any vamp that ever lifted lipstick.

Elsie Janis

Gossip

Am always a perfectly safe man to tell any dirt to,
as it goes in one ear and out my mouth.

Ernest Hemingway

Government

The government is the only known vessel that
leaks from the top.

James Reston

Grammar

"Whom are you?" he said, for he had been to
night school.

George Ade

"Shut up," he explained.

Ring Lardner

Gravity

It's a good thing there's gravity or else when birds died, they'd stay where they were.

Steven Wright

Guidebooks

In 1945 an Italian-English phrase book was hastily compiled in Florence to promote a better understanding between the Florentines and British and American troops. It contained the following entry.

ITALIAN	ENGLISH
Posso presentare il conte.	Meet the cunt.

W. H. Auden

Gynecology

A male gynecologist is like an auto mechanic who has never owned a car.

Carrie Snow

Haircut

Why don't you get a haircut? You look like a Chrysanthemum.

P.G. Wodehouse

Handshake

I shook Milton Wohl's small, damp hand—imagine squeezing a pork kidney.

Andrew Bregman

Happiness

I have to tell you something. I cannot help being happy. I've struggled against it but no good. Apart from an old five minutes here and there, I have been happy all my life. There is, I am well aware, no virtue whatever in this. It results from a combination of heredity, health, good fortune, and shallow intellect.

Arthur Marshall

Harpsichord

The harpsichord sounds like two skeletons copulating on a corrugated iron roof—in a thunderstorm.

Sir Thomas Beecham

Health Care

I think, said Mr. Dooley, that if th' Christyan Scientists had some science an' th' doctors more Christianity, it wudden't make anny diff'rence which ye called in—if ye had a good nurse.

Finley Peter Dunne

This warning from the New York City Department of Health

Fraud: Be suspicious of any doctor who tries to take your temperature with his finger.

David Letterman

History/Historians

A historian is often only a journalist facing backwards.

Karl Kraus

Holland

Apart from cheese and tulips, the main product of the country is advocaat, a drink made from lawyers.

Alan Coren

Hollywood

Hollywood money isn't money. It's congealed snow, melts in your hands, and there you are.

Dorothy Parker

The only "ism" Hollywood believes in is plagiarism.

Dorothy Parker

Working for Warner Bros. is like fucking a porcupine; it's a hundred pricks against one.

Wilson Mizener

The son-in-law always rises.

William Goldman

You can seduce a man's wife in Hollywood, attack his daughter and wipe your hands on his canary, but if you don't like his movie you're dead.

Joseph Von Sternberg

Behind the phoney tinsel of Hollywood lies the real tinsel.

Oscar Levant

Home Owners

The fellow who owns his own home is always coming out of a hardware store.

Kin Hubbard

Horses

I know two things about the horse, and one of them is rather coarse.

Anonymous

Mr. Polly wondered what the horse thought of him and whether it really liked being held and patted on the neck, or whether it only submitted out of contempt.

H. G. Wells

If the world were a logical place, men would ride side-saddle.

Rita Mae Brown

Horses and jockeys mature earlier than people—which is why horses are admitted to race tracks at the age of two and jockeys before they are old enough to shave.

Dick Beddoes

Hot Dogs

Do you know what I love most about baseball?
The pine tar, the resin, the grass, the dirt—and
that's just in the hot dogs.

David Letterman

Human Condition

Your whole being is involved in taking care of
someone else, worrying about what they think of
you, how they treat you, how you can make them
treat you better. Right now everyone in the world
seems to think that they are codependent and that
they come from dysfunctional families. They call
it codependency. I call it the human condition.

Cynthia Heimel

Humanity

Strange as it may sound, among all the millions of countenances with two eyes, a nose in the middle, and a mouth below it, no two precisely resemble each other.

E. V. Lucas

Humor

Good taste and humor are a contradiction in terms, like a chaste whore.

Malcolm Muggeridge

Hungary/Hungarians

A Hungarian would sell his grandmother—but couldn't be trusted to deliver.

Anthony Powell

One Hungarian genius sees another Hungarian genius not as a genius, but as a Hungarian.

Emeric Pressburger, on Alex Korda

If there are ten Hungarians there are twenty opinions.

Folk saying

Any time you see a Hungarian, kick him. He'll know why.

Anonymous

Hunting

When a man wants to murder a tiger he calls it sport; when a tiger wants to murder him he calls it ferocity.

George Bernard Shaw

One knows so well the popular idea of health. The English country gentleman galloping after a fox— the unspeakable in full pursuit of the uneatable.

Oscar Wilde

103

I ask people why they have deer heads on their walls, and they say, "Because it's such a beautiful animal." There you go. Well, I think my mother's attractive, but I have *photographs* of her.

Ellen DeGeneres

Hygiene

I am constantly amazed when I talk to young people to learn how much they know about sex and how little about soap.

Billie Burke

Hypocrisy

I hope you have not been leading a double life, pretending to be wicked and really being good all the time. That would be hypocrisy.

Oscar Wilde

A hypocrite is a person who . . . but who isn't?

Don Marquis

Ice Cream

I doubt whether the world holds for anyone a more soul-stirring surprise than the first adventure with ice-cream.

Heywood Broun

Ice-Skating

It has always seemed to me hard luck on the very best ice-dancing skaters that they have to spend so much of their time whizzing along backwards, with their bottoms sticking rather undecoratively out.

Arthur Marshall

Incest

The trouble with incest is that it gets you involved with relatives.

George S. Kaufman

Indecision

It's no exaggeration to say the undecideds could go one way or the other.

George Bush

Indifference

Sir, I view the proposal to hold an international exhibition at San Francisco with an equanimity bordering on indifference.

W. S. Gilbert

Insomnia

It is alleged by a friend of my family that I used to suffer from insomnia at the age of four, and that when she asked me how I managed to occupy my time at night I answered, "I lie awake and think about the past."

Ronald Knox

�’☙

Insults

The cruelest thing that has happened to Lincoln since being shot by Booth was to have fallen into the hands of Carl Sandburg.

Edmund Wilson

Mick Jagger has big lips. I saw him suck an egg out of a chicken. He can play a tuba from both ends. This man has got child-bearing lips.

Joan Rivers

You know, Sonny has a lot of good points. It's his bad points that aren't so good.

Sonny Liston's manager

- If there's ever a price on your head—take it!

- Why don't you go down to the morgue and tell them you're ready!

- Tell me, is that your lower lip or are you wearing a turtle-neck sweater?

- You've got a fine personality, Sir—but not for a human being!

- When he was born, his father came into the room and gave him a funny look. And as you can see, he's still got it!

- You're the sort of person Dr. Spooner would have called a shining wit!

- Will you please follow the example of your head and come to the point!

- That reminds me of a very funny story—will you take it from there, Sir?

- Why don't you move closer to the wall—that's plastered already!

- I'd like to help you out—tell me, which way did you come in?

- What exactly is on your mind? If you'll excuse the exaggeration?

- You've got a wonderful head on your shoulders. Tell me: whose is it?

Anonymous

I could eat alphabet soup and shit better lyrics.

Johnny Mercer, on a British musical

That guy was as sensitive as a goddam toilet seat.

J. D. Salinger

He's the only man I ever knew who had rubber pockets so he could steal soup.

Wilson Mizener, of a Hollywood studio chief

I've had a wonderful evening, but this wasn't it.

Groucho Marx, when leaving a party

Samuel Beckett once taught briefly at Campbell College, Belfast. When he was told that he was teaching the cream of the Ulster society he replied, "Yes, rich and thick."

I never forget a face, but in your case I'll make an exception.

Groucho Marx

Tommy Trinder gave me invaluable advice about hecklers. "Always get them to repeat what they have said," he told me, "because nothing sounds quite so funny or offensive when it is repeated."

Michael Bentine

Such an active lass. So outdoorsy. She loves nature in spite of what it did to her.

Bette Midler, on Princess Anne

No one can have a higher opinion of him than I have—and I think he's a dirty little beast.

W. S. Gilbert, on an old friend

When they circumcised Herbert Samuel they
threw away the wrong part.

David Lloyd George

I did not attend his funeral; but I wrote a nice letter saying I approved.

Mark Twain

I find Paul appealing and Peale appalling.

Adlai E. Stevenson, on American preacher
Norman Vincent Peale

[John F. Kennedy] is the enviably attractive
nephew who sings an Irish ballad for the company
and then winsomely disappears before the table-
clearing and dishwashing begin.

Lyndon B. Johnson

The Hon. Member disagrees. I can hear him shaking his head.

Pierre Elliott Trudeau

I have seen better organized creatures than you running around farmyards with their heads cut off.

John Cleese

He is so conceited that he will not even guess that we are saying how conceited he is.

A. G. MacDonald

Reader, suppose you were an idiot. And suppose you were a member of Congress. But I repeat myself.

Mark Twain

Frank Harris is not second rate nor third rate nor tenth rate, he is just his own horrible self.

George Bernard Shaw

Intellectuals

In France intellectuals are usually incapable of opening an umbrella.

Andre Malraux

Interviews

Broadway writer and wit Abe Burrows, during an amateur's interview, was asked "What was the low point of your career?" Burrows replied, "I hate to say so, kid, but I think this is it."

Invention

It may not be natural for a man to walk on two legs, but it was a noble invention.

Georg Christoph Lichtenberg

The airplane, the atomic bomb and the zipper have cured me of any tendency to state that a thing can't be done.

R. L. Duffus

Iowa

When you tell an Iowan a joke, you can see a kind of race going on between his brain and his expression.

Bill Bryson

Ireland/the Irish

The Irish are a nation of spoiled Prousts.

Flann O'Brien

Aunt Frieda was married to an Irishman *manqué*; he didn't drink, he didn't fight, he couldn't quote any Yeats.

Peter DeVries

He, I know not why, shewed upon all occasions an aversion to go to Ireland, where I proposed to him that we should make a tour.

JOHNSON: It is the last place where I should wish to travel?

BOSWELL: Should you not like to see Dublin, Sir?

JOHNSON: No Sir; Dublin is only a worse capital.

BOSWELL: Is not the Giant's Causeway worth seeing?

JOHNSON: Worth seeing? yes; but not worth going to see.

James Boswell

The actual Irish weather report is really a recording made in 1922, which no one has had occasion to change. "Scattered showers, periods of sunshine."

Wilfrid Sheed

If there were only three Irishmen in the world you'd find two of them in a corner talking about the other.

Brendan Behan

The tourist in Ireland has only to ask and he will be directed to something; whether or not it is what he things he is looking for.

Ciarán Carson

Only Irish coffee provides in a single glass all four essential food groups: alcohol, caffeine, sugar, and fat.

Alex Levine

Italians

I think the Italians are the best lovers in the world. They are quite likely to be inadequate when it comes to button-twiddling and so on. But the point is they create the ethos of being in love. They can also turn it off, of course. They are totally hypocritical. But that's all right. The important thing is not to let it be banal when it's happening—and they never do. They are utterly absorbed.

Germaine Greer

Jews

Mort Sahl, while attending a preview of Otto Preminger's film *Exodus*—stood up and called out, "Otto, let my people go!"

Journalism

The best headlines never fi

Bernard Levin

Journalism consists largely in saying "Lord Jones Dead" to people who never knew that Lord Jones was alive.

G. K. Chesterton

Rock journalism is people who can't write interviewing people who can't talk for people who can't read.

Frank Zappa

An editor is one who separates the wheat from the chaff and prints the chaff.

Adlai Stevenson

Judges

Judge: a law student who marks his own examination paper.

H.L. Mencken

Justice

The law, in its majestic equality, forbids the rich as well as the poor to sleep under bridges.

Anatole France

When I came back to Dublin, I was courtmartialled in my absence, and sentenced to death in my absence, so I said they could shoot me in my absence.

Brendan Behan

Kissing

He kissed her once by the pigsty when she wasn't looking and never kissed her again although she was looking all the time.

Dylan Thomas

He approached the substantial lips gingerly, as if edging into a swamp . . . They were wet and cold, like fresh fish.

Keith Waterhouse

Ladies

Being a lady war-correspondent is like being a lady wrestler—you can be one of them at a time, but not both simultaneously.

Dickey Chapelle

Language

Ms. is a syllable which sounds like a bumble bee breaking wind.

Hortense Calisher

That feller runs splendid but he needs help at the plate, which coming from the country chasing rabbits all winter give him strong legs, although he broke one falling out of a tree, which shows you can't tell, and when a curve ball comes he waves at it and if pitchers don't throw curves you have no pitching staff, so how is a manager going to know whether to tell boys to fall out of trees and break legs so he can fun fast even if he can't hit a curve ball?

Casey Stengel

So Harry says, "You don't like me any more. Why not?" And he says, "Because you've got so terribly pretentious." And Harry says, "Pretentious? *Moi?*"

John Cleese and Connie Booth

He put words into my mouth which I had to look up in the dictionary.

> *Graham Greene, on being interviewed by*
> *Anthony Burgess*

I am not like a lady at the court of Versailles, who said: 'What a dreadful pity that the bother at the Tower of Babel should have got language all mixed up, but for that, everyone would always have spoken French.

> *Voltaire*

Only kings, editors, and people with tapeworm have the right to use the editorial "we."

> *Mark Twain*

Fuck it, the fucking fucker's fucking fucked!

> *Anthony Burgess, quoting an army mechanic*
> *on his engine*

I've been in *Who's Who* and I know what's what, but it's the first time I ever made the dictionary!

> *Mae West, on the life jacket that was named in her honor*

She plunged into a sea of platitudes, and with the powerful breast stroke of a channel swimmer made her confident way towards the white cliffs of the obvious.

W. Somerset Maugham

Lord Ronald said nothing; he flung himself from the room, flung himself upon his horse and rode madly off in all directions.

Stephen Leacock

Last Words

I should never have switched from Scotch to Martinis.

Humphrey Bogart

This green wallpaper is killing me. Either it must go, or I shall.

Oscar Wilde

Las Vegas

It was not cafe society, it was Nescafe society.

Noel Coward

Laughter

She had a penetrating sort of laugh. Rather like a train going into a tunnel.

P. G. Wodehouse

Laundromats

If it weren't for laundromats half the letters in the United States would never get written.

Louis Phillips

Law Enforcement

I am advised that if a policeman ever warns me
that whatever I say will be taken down and
repeated in court, I should at once exclaim,
"Please, officer, don't hit me again."

Hugh Leonard

☞

Laws

There are two Newman's laws. The first one is "It
is useless to put on your brakes when your upside
down." The second is "Just when things look dark-
est, they go black."

Paul Newman

Lawsuits

I was never ruined but twice. Once when I lost a lawsuit and once when I won one.

Voltaire

Lawyers

Broke a mirror in my house and I'm supposed to get seven years bad luck, but my lawyer thinks he can get me five.

Steven Wright

What's black and white and brown and looks good on a lawyer? A doberman.

Mordecai Richler

Leisure

I'm prepared to take advice on leisure from Prince Philip. He's a world expert on leisure. He's been practicing for most of his adult life.

Neil Kinnock

Letter Writing

An offensive letter from a female American Catholic. I returned it to her husband with the note: "I shall be grateful if you will use whatever disciplinary means are customary in your country to restrain your wife from writing impertinent letters to men she doesn't know."

Evelyn Waugh

Life

Oh, isn't life a terrible thing, thank God!

Dylan Thomas

We're in a blessed drainpipe, and we've got to crawl along it till we die.

H. G. Wells

Lightning

There was an article somewhere a while ago about how to keep from getting hit by lightning. I don't remember too much about what it said, because our cook was reading a serial about a girl who fell in love with a jai-alai player, and took the magazine to bed with her every night, so that I didn't get very far with the lightning article except to learn that you mustn't stand around under trees, and I knew that already.

Wolcott Gibbs

Likes/Dislikes

Andrew Lloyd Webber complained to the late lyri-
cist Alan Jay Lerner, that some people dislike him
as soon as they meet him. "Perhaps that saves
time," Lerner mused.

Lingerie

Brevity is the soul of lingerie.
Dorothy Parker

Literature

Literature is mostly about sex and not much about having children and life is the other way round.

David Lodge

I always pulp my acquaintences before serving them up. You would never recognize a pig in a sausage.

Fanny Trollope

Many would have agreed with the Irish bishop who remarked that *Gulliver's Travels* seemed to be full of improbable statements, and that for his part he scarcely believed half of it.

Peter Costello

It was the kind of house-brick paperbound novels which records how the rape of a Choctaw squaw eventually leads to the foundation of a vast empire.

Clive James

Loneliness

The only thing that can make a woman feel lonelier than a vibrator can make her feel is a man.

Isha Elafi

Los Angeles

A city with all the personality of a paper cup.

Raymond Chandler

The difference between Los Angeles and yogurt is that yogurt has real culture.

Tom Taussik

Living in Los Angeles is like being a hemophiliac in a razor factory.

Robin Williams

Love

The second you meet someone that you're going to fall in love with you deliberately become a moron. You do this in order to fall in love, because it would be impossible to fall in love with a human being if you actually saw them for what they are.

Fran Lebowitz

Love: An agreement on the part of two people to overestimate each other.

E. M. Cioran

Lovemaking

How alike are the groans of love to those of the dying.

Malcolm Lowry

Luck

Watch out when you're getting all you want; fattening hogs ain't in luck.

Joel Chandler Harris

He is so unlucky that he runs into accidents which start out to happen to somebody else.

Don Marquis

Lying

Our whole lives are lived in a tangle of telling, not telling, misleading, allowing to know, concealing, eavesdropping and collusion. When Washington said he could not tell a lie, his father must have answered, "You had better learn."

Germaine Greer

Marriage

Before getting married, find out if you're really in love—Ask yourself, "Would I mind getting financially destroyed by this person?"

Johnny Carson

A new bride should be treated like a new car. Keep her steady on the straight, watch out for warning lights on the ignition and lubrication panels and when you reckon she's run in, give her all you've got.

Auberon Waugh

No married man is genuinely happy if he has to drink worse whiskey than he used to drink when he was single.

H. L. Mencken

Mrs. Hall of Sherbourne was brought to bed yesterday of a dead child, some weeks before she expected, owing to a fright. I suppose she happened to look unawares at her husband.

Jane Austen

I've married a few people I shouldn't have, but haven't we all?

Mamie Van Doren

Bigamy is having one husband too many. Monogamy is the same.

Anonymous, quoted in Erica Jong's Fear of Flying

To speak frankly, I am not in favor of long engagements. They give people the opportunity of finding out about each other's character before marriage, which I think is never advisable.

Oscar Wilde

I want to get as thin as my first husband's promises.

Texas Guinan

Marriage has teeth, and him bite very hot.

Jamaican proverb

Never marry a woman who has extensive knowledge of nautical knots and can tie over 200 knots.

Lewis Grizzard

Chumps always make the best husbands. When you marry, Sally, grab a chump. Tap his head first, and if it rings solid, don't hesitate.

P. G. Wodehouse

We in the industry know that behind every successful screenwriter stands a woman. And behind her stands his wife.

Groucho Marx

There is a vast difference between the savage and the civilized man, but it is never apparent to their wives after breakfast.

Helen Rowland

I don't know if it's good for baseball but it sure beats the hell out of rooming with Phil Rizzuto!

Yogi Berra, on the marriage of Joe DiMaggio and Marilyn Monroe

I got married the second time in the way that, when a murder is committed, crackpots turn up at the police station to confess the crime.

Delmore Schwartz

Some people ask the secret of our long marriage. We take time to go to a restaurant two times a week. A little candlelight dinner, soft music and dancing. She goes Tuesdays, I go Fridays.

Henny Youngman

The trouble with marrying your mistress is that you create a job vacancy.

Sir James Goldsmith

Masturbation

Of all the various kinds of sexual intercourse this has the least to recommend it. As an amusement it is too fleeting. As an occupation it is too wearing. As a public exhibition there is no money in it. It is unsuited to the drawing room.

Mark Twain

Medicine

Randolph Churchill went into a hospital . . . to have a lung removed. It was announced that the trouble was not "malignant" . . . it was a typical triumph of modern science to find the only part of Randolph that was not malignant and remove it.

Evelyn Waugh

The desire to take medicine is perhaps the greatest feature which distinguishes man from animals.

William Osler

I would have thought it would at least be easier to remember (or even check) whether you had or had not inserted a suppository than it is to remember if you've swallowed a pill.

Katherine Whitehorn

Memory

When I was younger, I could remember anything whether it had happened or not; but my faculties are decaying now and soon I shall be so that I cannot remember anything but the things that never happened. It is sad to go to pieces like this but we all have to do it.

Mark Twain

Men

It is a well-documented fact that guys will not ask for directions. This is a biological thing. This is why it takes several million sperm cells, each one wriggling in its own direction, totally confident it knows where it is going, to locate a female egg, despite the fact that the egg is, relative to them, the size of Wisconsin.

Dave Barry

My ancestors wandered in the wilderness for 40 years because even in biblical times, men would not stop to ask for directions.

Elayne Boosler

All men are afraid of eyelash curlers. They don't understand them, and they don't want to get near them. I sleep with one under my pillow, instead of a gun.

Rita Rudner

He was so ugly, honest to goodness, he hurt my feelings.

Moms Mabley

The American male doesn't mature until he has exhausted all other possibilities.

Wilfrid Sheed

I've never found brawn appealing. If I went out with Macho Man I think I'd have a permanent headache. Kind of 'You Tarzan—Mi-graine.'

Overheard on a bus, quoted in Judy Allen's
Picking on Men

It is always now said that puny men are pugnacious because of the greater harm they could do if powerful.

Evelyn Waugh

Mexico

Mexicans have always asked themselves why a people so close to God should be so near the United States.

Carlos Fuentes

Miracles

Everything is miraculous. It is miraculous that one does not melt in one's bath.

Pablo Picasso

Money

Money doesn't grow on trees, and if it did, somebody else would own the orchard.

Lewis Grizzard

Stop babbling, man! How much?

William Butler Yeats, on hearing by phone that he had won the Nobel Prize (attrib.)

Mothers-In-Law

Behind every successful man stands a surprised mother-in-law.

Hubert Humphrey

Mottos

National motto of Lilliput: Every King an Inch.

John T. Winterich

✔

Movies

David Lean showed the film *Brief Encounter* to a Rochester audience at the time of its release; they found it hilarious and baffling, and shouted "isn't 'e ever goin' to 'ave it orf with 'er"?

Philip Hensler

Gandhi was everything the voting members of the Academy would like to be: moral, tan, and thin.

Joe Morgenstern

The movie business is macabre, grotesque. It is a combination of a football game and a brothel.

Federico Fellini

"Bring on the empty horses!"

Shouted direction by Hungarian-born Michael Curtiz, for one hundred riderless horses. Scene in "The Charge of the Light Brigade." This direction broke up stars David Niven and Errol Flynn, who laughed uproariously, to which Curtiz angrily responded:

"You and your stinking language! You think I know fuck nothing. Well, let me tell you, I know fuck all!"

"If the dead were to come back,
What would you do with them?

Alfred Hitchcock

You would call them *Topaz.*

from Time *Magazine's review of Hitchcock's movie*

Murder

There are only about twenty murders a year in London and many not at all serious—some are just husbands killing their wives.

Commander G. H. Hatherhill of Scotland Yard, 1954

Music

Classical music is the kind we keep thinking will turn into a tune.

Kin Hubbard

The Music teacher came once a week to bridge the awful gap between Dorothy and Chopin.

George Ade

The tuba is certainly the most intestinal of instruments, the very lower bowel of music.

Peter DeVries

Extraordinary how potent cheap music is.
Noel Coward

To Jack (my husband), his violin is comfort and
relaxation. To his inky wife, it's time to put her
head down the waste disposal unit.
Maureen Lipman

That made the buggers hop!
*Sir Thomas Beecham, after conducting a ballet at twice
the normal speed*

If you can imagine a man having a vasectomy
without anesthetic to the sound of frantic sitar-
playing, you will have some idea what popular
Turkish music is like.
Bill Bryson

Composers should not think too much—it inter-
feres with their plagiarism.
Howard Dietz

Without music, life would be a mistake.
Friedrich Wilhelm Nietzsche

We cannot expect you to be with us all the time, but perhaps you could be good enough to keep in touch now and again.
Sir Thomas Beecham, to player in his orchestra

Music hath charms to soothe the savage breast; unfortunately, there seem to be more savage breasts than ever before.
Louis Phillips

There are two golden rules for an orchestra: start together and finish together. The public doesn't give a damn what goes on in between.
Sir Thomas Beecham

My favorite song title: "I Can't Get Over You Until You Get Out From Under Him."
Lewis Grizzard

Beethoven's Fifth Symphony may be Fate—or Kate—knocking at the door. That is up to you.

C. B. Rees

Twentieth-century music is like pedophilia. No matter how persuasively and persistently its champions urge their cause, it will never be accepted by the public at large, who will continue to regard it with incomprehension, outrage and repugnance.

Kingsley Amis

Name Dropping

I mustn't go singling out names. One must not be a name-dropper, as Her Majesty remarked to me yesterday.

Norman St. John Stevas

Names

Mrs. Patrick Campbell was seated next to Joseph Schildkraut at a Hollywood dinner party. She remarked that he was a handsome young man, and should try being an actor. "But, madam," he replied, "I am Joseph Schildkraut." "Oh, well," she said, "You can always change your name."

Wendell Phillips. He was about the only Bostonian of his time who wore no middle name and he was therefore considered half naked.

Frank Sullivan

Said Jerome K. Jerome to Ford Madox Ford,
'There's something, old boy, that I've always
abhorred: when people address me and
call me' Jerome.' Are they being standoffish,
 or too much at home?"
Said Ford, "I agree; It's the same thing with me."

William Cole

Nationality

There have been many definitions of hell, but for the English the best definition is that it is a place where the Germans are the police, the Swedish are the comedians, the Italians are the defense force, Frenchmen dig the roads, the Belgians are the pop singers, the Turks cook the food, the Irish are the waiters, the Greeks run the government and the common language is Dutch.

David Frost and Antony Jay

Germans are flummoxed by humor, the Swiss have no concept of fun, the Spanish think there is nothing ridiculous about eating dinner at midnight, and the Italians should never, ever been let in on the invention of the motor car.

Bill Bryson

The Englishman is never happy unless he is miserable; a Scotsman is never at home but when he is abroad; an Irishman is never at peace but when he's fighting.

Anonymous

In America only the successful writer is important, in France all writers are important, in England no writer is important, and in Australia you have to explain what a writer is.

Geoffrey Cottrell

Somebody should tell the Germans about hyphens.

William Cole

An Englishman thinks seated; a Frenchman standing; an American pacing; an Irishman afterward.

Nature

To me the outdoors is what you must pass through in order to get from your apartment into a taxicab.

Fran Lebowitz

Now, nature, as I am only too well aware, has her enthusiasts, but on the whole, I am not to be counted among them. To put it rather bluntly, I am not the type who wants to go back to the land; I am the type who wants to go back to the hotel.

Fran Lebowitz

Newspapers

Newspapers have roughly the same relationship to life as fortune-tellers to metaphysics.

Karl Kraus

Saying the *Washington Post* is just a newspaper is like saying Rasputin was just a country priest.

Patrick J. Buchanan during the Watergate investigations

New York

WILLIAMS: Next thing I knew, I was in New York.

INTERVIEWER: Was that a heavy adjustment for you to make?

WILLIAMS: I was the walking epitome of fur*shirr* meets yo'ass. On my first day in New York, I went to school dressed like a typical California kid: I wore tie-up yoga pants and a Hawaiian shirt, and I kept stepping in dog shit with my thongs.

Robin Williams

New York is like my Lourdes, where I go for spiritual refreshment . . . a place where you're least likely to be bitten by a wild goat.

Brendan Behan

New Zealand

If an English nanny and an English butler sat down to design a country, they would come up with New Zealand.

Anonymous

Nonsense

What we want today is social reform, tariff reform and, more than likely, chloroform. What did Gladstone say after ninety-nine? Why, a hundred of course—and he was right.

Billy Bennett

Norway/The Norwegians

I don't like Norwegians at all. The sun never sets, the bar never opens, and the whole country smells of kippers.

Evelyn Waugh

Noses

I attended a dinner party in Moscow at which the host pointed out that the two teenage daughters at table with us were much alike. I saw no resemblance until he said that they both had noses like soldering irons.

Alex de Jong

Nostalgia

Nothing is more responsible for the good old days than a bad memory.

Franklin Pierce Adams

Novels

When somebody in a novel says something like "I've never been in an air crash," you know this means that five minutes later they will be.

Alan Bennett

Oceans

Sponges grow in the ocean. I wonder how much deeper the ocean would be would be if that didn't happen.

Steven Wright

Old Age

I am just turning forty and taking my time about it.
> *Harold Lloyd at seventy-seven, when asked his age*

The misery of a child is interesting to a mother, the misery of a young man is interesting to a young woman, the misery of an old man is interesting to no one.
> *Victor Hugo*

The doctors say I'm a very interesting case and generally patronise my belly—to think that I used to write *Playboy*; MacKenna, and now I'm just a bunch of interesting bowels.
> *John Millington Synge, in a letter to Stephen MacKenna*

A beard creates lice, not brains.
> *Ammianus*

I'm as old as my tongue and a little older than my teeth.
> *Jonathan Swift*

You get old, first you forget names, then you forget faces, then you forget to zip your fly, then you forget to unzip your fly.

Branch Rickey

I used to have four supple members and one stiff one. Now I have four stiff ones and one supple one.

Duc De Morny

Opera

She was the kind of singer who had to take any note above A with her eyebrows.

Montagu Glass

Joan Sutherland will sing only if her husband conducts, so I accept the old Viennese saying that if you want the meat, you have to take the bones.

Rudolf Bing

Parsifal is the kind of opera that starts at six o'clock. After it has been going three hours, you look at your watch and it says 6:20.

David Randolph

The opera is like a husband with a foreign title: expensive to support, hard to understand, and therefore a supreme social challenge.

Cleveland Amory

My experience with opera has been limited because of Nature's shortsightedness in the construction of the horse. Horses are simply not powerful enough to drag me into the presence of all that hog calling.

H. Allen Smith

Of one thing I am firmly convinced, and that is that you must either get married or write an opera. One would do you just about as much good—or harm !—as the other.

Richard Wagner

Opinions

Nothing is more conducive to peace of mind than not having any opinion at all.

Georg Christoph

👀

Painting

I suppose Manet's famous *Dejuner sur l'Herbe* was a picnic within the meaning of the act, and whatever those glum-looking men in Sunday attire were up to with that naked lady in their midst, it certainly wasn't roughing it.

Humphrey Lyttelton

Pantomime

In my youth, I wanted to be a great pan-
tomimist—but I found I had nothing to say.

Victor Borge

Paradoxes

Soderquist's Paradox: There are more horses' asses
than there are horses.

John Peer

Parents/Parenting

A suburban mother's role is to deliver children
obstetrically once, and by car forever after.

Peter De Vries

The worse waste of breath, next to playing a saxophone, is advising a son.

Kin Hubbard

If you've never seen a real, fully developed look of disgust, just tell your son how you conducted yourself when you were a boy.

Kin Hubbard

Parody

Early to rise and early to bed makes a male healthy and wealthy and dead.

James Thurber

Parts of Speech

I lately lost a preposition:
It hid, I thought beneath my chair.
And angrily I cried: 'Perdition!'
Up from out of in under there!

Morris Bishop

Paternity

That was when you were only a worried look on
your father's face.

Anonymous

Patriotism

"My country right or wrong," is a thing no patriot would think of saying except in a desperate case. It is like saying, "My mother, drunk or sober!"

G. K. Chesterton

Patrons

Is not a patron, my Lord, one who looks with unconcern on a man struggling for life in the water, and when he has reached ground, encumbers him with help?

Samuel Johnson, letter to the Earl of Chesterfield

Peanut Butter

. . . I forgot to tell you about the strange chat I overheard in the West Suffolk Hospital in Bury St. Edmonds. In the next cubicle a small boy was having his ears syringed out and being quizzed by a doctor. It transpired that while he had been fast asleep the night before, his brother crept into his room and filled his ears with peanut butter. I knew there must be some use for the stuff.

Jeffrey Bernard

Philanthropy

It is difficult to love mankind unless one has a reasonable private income, and when one has a reasonable private income one has better things to do than loving mankind.

Hugh Kingsmill

Philosophy

Life is what happens when you are making other plans.

John Lennon

Nothing is impossible for the man who doesn't have to do it himself.

A. H. Weiler

Thought: Why does man kill? He kills for food. And not only food: frequently there must be a beverage.

Woody Allen

"One lives and learns, doesn't one?"
"That is certainly one of the more prevalent delusions."

Noel Coward

Life is like a dog-sled team. If you ain't the lead dog, the scenery never changes.

Lewis Grizzard

More than any time in history mankind faces a crossroads. One path leads to despair and utter hopelessness, the other to total extinction. Let us pray that we have the wisdom to choose correctly.

Woody Allen

Being born is like being kidnapped. And then sold into slavery.

Andy Warhol

Life. It's full of such sadness and sorrow, sometimes I think it's better not to be born at all! . . . But how many people do you meet in a lifetime who were that lucky?

Yiddish saying

Life is something you do when you can't go to sleep.

Fran Lebowitz

Philosophy is the art of bewildering oneself methodically.

Heathiana

I think I think; therefore, I think I am.
Ambrose Bierce

I cheated on the final of my metaphysics exam; I looked into the soul of the boy sitting next to me.
Woody Allen

If Shaw and Einstein couldn't beat death, what chance have I got? Practically none.
Mel Brooks

Do you believe in a life to come?
Mine has always been just that.
Samuel Beckett

Phobias

Tell us your phobias and we will tell you what you are afraid of.
Robert Benchley

Playwriting

With plays you only have to fill the center of the page. Novels take a tremendous amount of typing.
Paul Rudnick

The reason why Absurdist plays take place in No Man's land with only two characters is mainly financial.

Arthur Adamov

Poets/Poetry

Li Po wrote poems on rice paper and floated them down rivers until they sank out of sight. Contemporary poets publish their poems in little magazines. The results are much the same.

Louis Phillips

A poet's hope: to be
like some valley cheese,
local, but prized elsewhere.

W.H. Auden, "Shorts"

Poison

No Roman was ever able to say, "I dined last night with the Borgias."

Max Beerbohm

Poker

One night I stayed up all night playing poker with tarot cards. I got a full house and four people died.

Steven Wright

Politics/Politicians

One day all the don't-knows will get in, and then where will we be?

Spike Milligan, about a pre-election poll

Boys, I may not know much, but I know chicken shit from chicken salad.

Lyndon B. Johnson, on a speech by Richard Nixon

Give a member of Congress a junket and a mimeograph machine and he thinks he is Secretary of State.

Dean Rusk

Render any politician down and there's enough fat to fry an egg.

Spike Milligan

A reformer is a guy who rides through a sewer in a glass-bottomed boat.

James J. Walker

Dealing with the State Department is like watching an elephant become pregnant.

Franklin Delano Roosevelt

Dealing with the Russians is like trying to play music through an ultrasonic dog whistle.

Yugoslav Diplomat (1970)

Reader, suppose you were an idiot; and suppose you were a member of congress; but I repeat myself.

Mark Twain

The best reason I can think of for not running for President of the United States is that you have to shave twice a day.

Adlai Stevenson

Mothers all want their sons to grow up to be Pres ident, but they don't want them to become politi- cians in the process.

John F. Kennedy

Th' prisidincy is th' highest office in th' gift iv th' people. Th' vice-prisidincy is th' next highest an' th' lowest It isn't a crime exactly. Ye can't be sint to jail f'r it, but it's a kind iv a disgrace. It's like writin' anonymous letters.

Finley Peter Dunne

A statesman is any politician it's considered safe to name a school after.

Bill Vaughan

Democrats are the kind of people who'd stop to help you change a flat, but would somehow manage to set your car on fire. I would be reluctant to entrust them a Cuisinart, let alone the economy. The Republicans, on the other hand, would know how to fix your tire, but they wouldn't bother to stop because they'd want to be on time for Ugly Pants Night at the country club.

Dave Barry

There are some politicians who, if their constituents were cannibals, would promise them missionaries for dinner.

H. L. Mencken

Population

South Dakota is so underpopulated that merely by entering it you become a member of the state legislature.

Dave Barry

Portraits

A portrait is a picture in which there is something wrong with the mouth.

Eugene Speicher

Postage

Fifteen cents of every twenty–cent stamp goes for storage.

Louis Rukeyser

Poverty

There is one advantage of being poor–a doctor will cure you faster.

Kin Hubbard

Pride

A confessional passage has probably never been written that didn't stink a little bit of the writer's pride in having given up his pride.

J. D. Salinger

Promptness

I've been on a calendar, but never on time.

Marilyn Monroe

Proverbs

Only a fool tests the depth of the water with both feet.

African proverb

An apple a day, if aimed straight, keeps the doctor away.

P. G. Wodehouse

When the prick stands, the brains get buried in the ground.

Yiddish proverb

You cannot get blood from a stone, but you can get a government grant to try.

Louis Phillips

He who has butter on his head should not walk in the sun.

Yiddish proverb

He who carries elephants upon his back should be careful not to step on crickets.

African proverb

Psychology

The only reason I never worked as a psychologist is that, as Voltaire said of priests, I cannot understand why when two psychologists meet in the street, they don't both of them burst out laughing.

Anonymous

A neurotic is the man who builds a castle in the air. A psychotic is the man who lives in it—and a psychiatrist is the man who collects the rent.

Lord Webb-Johnson

These modern analysts, they charge so much! In my day, for five marks Freud himself would treat you. For ten marks he would treat you and press your pants. For fifteen marks Freud would let *you* treat *him*—and that included a choice of any two vegetables.

Woody Allen

Public Speaking

I do not object to people looking at their watches
when I am speaking. But I do strongly object
when they start shaking them to make sure they
are still going.

Lord Birkett

Before I begin my speech, I have something to say.

Ambassador Robert Straus

Tell 'em what you're going to tell 'em; then tell
'em; then tell 'em what you told 'em.

Anonymous advice to public speakers

When a man is asked to make a speech, the first
thing he has to decide is what to say.

Gerald Ford

The sanity of the average banquet speaker lasts
about two and a half months; at the end of that
time he begins to mutter to himself, and calls out
in his sleep.

James Thurber

Publishing

To publish an anthology is to turn oneself into a pheasant on the first day of August.

Edward Lucie-Smith

Having been unpopular in high school is not just cause for book publication.

Fran Lebowitz

Publishing a book is like farting at a party—you have to wait till people stop looking at you before you can start acting normally again.

Philip Larkin

Punctuation

The exclamation mark is the literary equivalent of a man holding up a card reading LAUGHTER to a studio audience.

Miles Kingston

Puns

Some of my plays peter out and some pan out.
J. M. Barrie

Though he might be more humble, there is no police like Holmes.
E.W. Hornung

Thou canst not serve both cod and salmon.
Ada Leverson, on being offered a choice of fish at a dinner party

I speak more in Seurat than in Ingres.
Charles Poore, reviewing French art book

25 September. Gore Vidal is being interviewed on "Start the Week" along with Richard ("Watership Down") Adams. Adams is asked what he thought of Vidal's new novel about Lincoln. "I thought it was meretricious." "Really?" says Gore. "Well, meretricious and a happy new year." That's the way to do it.

Alan Bennett

Ladies and Gentleman, I give you a toast. It is "Absinthe makes the tart grow fonder."

Hugh Drummond

The amoeba contributed almost nothing to the development of love—unless you want to consider that trivial song, "Amoeba Wrong, But I Think You're Wonderful."

Groucho Marx

Mother always told me my day was coming, but I never realized that I'd end up being the shortest knight of the year.

Gordon Richards, British jockey, on getting his knighthood

Live music is an anachronism, and now is the winter of our discotheque.

Benny Greene

"Ah, the unbearable likeness of Behan!"

Phelin Donlon, on viewing a photograph of Brendan Behan in the lobby of Dublin's Abbey Theatre

What on earth's this?
A piece of cod, sir.
A piece of cod which passeth all understanding.

(Attr.) Sir Edward Lutyens, to a waiter at Brooks'

The trouble with Verlaine was he was always chasing Rimbauds.

Dorothy Parker

Beating his chest, the Laird of the Manor said to the country lassie, "Me tartan, you plain."

William Cole

A thief has been stealing wine by cutting round holes in vinters' windows—and then working his fingers to the Beaune.

Punch

The Queen

The night that I slept with the Queen
She said as I whispered *Ich dien:*
"This is royalty's night out,
So please switch the light out,
The Queen may be had but not seen."

Dylan Thomas (attrib.)

Quotations

Don't make up classical quotations—that's digging
up your grandmother in front of your mistress.

Leon-Paul Fargue

Rain

If I were running the world I would have it rain
only between 2 and 5 A.M. Anyone who was out
then ought to get wet.

William Lyon Phelps

Reading

. . . reading of any kind is on the decline. Half the
American people never read a newspaper. Half
never vote for President. One hopes it is the same
half.

Gore Vidal

I have just read a long novel by Henry James.
Much of it made me think of the priest con-
demned for a long space to confess nuns.

Jack Butler Yeats

I have read only one book in my life, and that is *White Fang.* It's so frightfully good I've never bothered to read another.

Nancy Mitford

Sartor Resartus is simply unreadable, and for me that always sort of spoils a book.

Will Cuppy

ᦉ

Ronald Reagan

In a disastrous fire in President Reagan's library both books were destroyed. And the real tragedy is that he hadn't finished coloring one.

Jonathan Hunt

Religion

If Jesus was a Jew, why the Spanish name?

Bill Maher

If I had been the Virgin Mary, I would have said, "no."

Stevie Smith

The organs of human utterance are too frail to describe my lack of interest in papal affairs.

George Lyttelton

There's the story that, when Groucho Marx encountered a bishop in an elevator who said to him "Thank you for all the pleasure you've given people over forty years," Groucho replied, "And thank you, your eminence, for all the misery you've caused thousands of people over the centuries."

I have noticed again and again since I have been in the church that lay interest in ecclesiastic matters is a prelude to insanity.

Evelyn Waugh

But as for helping me in the outside world, the convent taught me only that if you spit on a pencil eraser it will erase ink. . . . I was fired from there, finally, for a lot of things, among them my insistence that the Immaculate Conception was spontaneous combustion.

Dorothy Parker

God sneezed. What could I say to Him?

Henny Youngman

"Important if true." Inscription which Kinglake wanted on all churches.

Geoffrey Madan

Holy Moses! Have a look!
Flesh decayed in every nook!
Some rare bits of brain lie here,
Mortal loads of beef and beer . . .

Amanda Ros, words on visiting Westminster Abbey

My theology, briefly, is that the universe was dictated but not signed.

Christopher Morley

We must respect the other fellow's religion, but only in the sense and to the extent that we respect his theory that his wife is beautiful and his children smart.

H. L. Mencken

It was just one of those parties that got out of hand.

Lenny Bruce, the crucifixion

Why is it when we talk to God, we're said to be praying—but when God talks to us, we're schizophrenic.

Lily Tomlin

I was a very wicked child. I had a praying mantis that I converted to an agnostic.

Bill Cosby

Replies

A friend at the Algonquin, passing behind Marc Connelly's chair, rubs his hand over Marc's bald head, saying, "I like your bald head, Marc. It feels just like my wife's behind."

Connelly, rubbing his hand reflectively over his baldness, replies, "So it does, Max, so it does."

Mr. Ball? How very singular.
Sir Thomas Beecham

"Are you lost, daddy?" I asked tenderly. "Shut up," he explained.
Ring Lardner

Asked what would have happened if Kruschev had been assassinated rather than Kennedy, Sir Alec Douglas-Home replied, "I doubt that Aristotle Onassis would have married Mrs. Kruschev."

Resolutions

New Year's Resolution:
1. To refrain from saying witty, unkind things, unless they are really witty and irreparably damaging.
2. To tolerate fools more gladly, provided this does not encourage them to take up more of my time.

James Agate

Restaurants

I've known what it is to be hungry, but I always went right to a restaurant.

Ring Lardner

The disparity between a restaurant's price and food quality rises in direct proportion to the size of the pepper mill.

Bryan Miller

Royalty

Finding, however, that he was not memorable, he very patriotically abdicated in favor of Henry IV, Part II.

W. C. Sellar and R. J. Yeatman

Sacrifice

She's the sort of woman who lives for others—you can always tell the others by their hunted expression.

C. S. Lewis

Sailing

I had a friend whose boyfriend insisted on taking her sailing. She said she didn't mind being terribly wet, or cold, or hungry, or seasick, or frightened. She just didn't like them all at once.

Dick Francis

Scandal

Mme. de Genlis, in order to avoid the scandal of coquetry, always yielded easily.

Science

The rule of accuracy: When working toward the solution of a problem it always helps if you know the answer.

John Peer

Scotland/The Scottish

It requires a surgical operation to get a joke well into a Scotch understanding. Their only idea of wit . . . is laughing immoderately at stated intervals.

Reverend Sydney Smith

Sir, the noblest prospect that Scotchmen ever sees is the high road that leads him to London.

Samuel Jonhson

The Scots are incapable of considering their literary geniuses purely as writers or artists. Thy must be either an excuse for a glass or a text for the next sermon.

George Malcolm Thomson

It is never difficult to distinguish between a Scotsman with a grievance and a ray of sunshine.

P.G. Wodehouse

Screen Writing

I'm a Hollywood writer; so I put on a sports jacket and take off my brain.

Ben Hecht

It's slave labor and what do you get for it? A lousy fortune.

S.N. Berhrman

What we want is a story that starts with an earthquake and works its way up to a climax.

Samuel Goldwyn

I worked on fourteen different stories before a single line of mine ever turned up on the screen. And then it wasn't much of a line. It was nothing more than a policeman walking into a scene and saying, 'Get along with yez now.' The way I had it was, 'Now, get along with yez.' They changed it on me, but the words were mine. They'll kill you!"

Robert Benchley

194

Sermons

When I hear a man preach, I like to see him act
as if he were fighting bees.

Abraham Lincoln

Self-Description

I love talking about nothing. It is the only thing I
know anything about.

Oscar Wilde

If I asked for a cup of coffee, someone would
search for the double meaning.

Mae West

I am the type of guy who'd sell you a rat's asshole
for a wedding ring.

Tom Waits

I am told I am a true cosmopolitan. I am unhappy everywhere.

Stephen Vizinczey

Let me have my own way in exactly everything, and a sunnier and pleasanter creature does not exist.

Thomas Carlyle

I used to be Snow White—but I drifted.

Mae West

Yes, I am exactly like the characters in my books. I am very tough and have been known to break a Vienna roll with my bare hands. I am very handsome, have a powerful physique and change my shirt every Monday.

Raymond Chandler

I was the toast of two continents—Greenland and Australia.

Dorothy Parker

Twenty-four years ago I was strangely handsome. The remains of it are still visible through the rifts of time. I was so handsome that human activities ceased as if spellbound when I came into view, and even inanimate things stopped to look—like locomotives and district messenger boys and so on. In San Francisco in the rainy season I was often taken for fair weather.

Mark Twain

I am, in point of fact, a particularly haughty and exclusive person of pre-Adamite ancestral descent. You will understand this when I tell you that I can trace my ancestry back to a proto-plasmal primordial atomic globule. Consequently, my family pride is something inconceivable. I can't help it. I was born sneering.

W. S. Gilbert

I don't have to look up my family tree, because I know that I'm the sap.

Fred Allen

I'm no different from anybody else with two arms, two legs, and forty-two hundred hits.

Pete Rose

Under a forehead roughly comparable to that of a Javanese and Piltdown man are visible a pair of tiny pig eyes, lit up alternately by greed and concupiscence.

S. J. Perelman, self-description

The mome rath isn't born that could outgrabe me.

Nicol Williamson

Take a close-up photograph of me! You might as well use a picture of a relief map of Ireland!

Nancy Astor

Self-Love

There's no one, no one, loves you like yourself.
Brendan Behan

Sermons

Did you hear of the parson who began his sermon,
"As God said—and rightly—"? It grows on you.
Rupert Hart-Davis

Servants

Servants should not be ill. We have quite enough
illnesses of our own without them adding to the
symptoms.

Lady Diana Cooper

But that is not because the hero is no hero, but
because the valet is valet.

Friedrich Nietzsche

Sex

If all the girls attending it (the Yale prom) were
laid end to end, I wouldn't be surprised.

Dorothy Parker

I have done almost every human activity inside a
taxi which does not require main drainage.

Alan Brien

what in hell
have i done to deserve
all these kittens

Don Marquis

A man is as old as the woman he feels.

Groucho Marx

A one-time U.S. Ambassador in Europe, astonishing in view of his age, is said to have approached all problems with a closed mind and an open fly.

John Kenneth Galbraith

It is said of me that when I was young I divided my time impartially among wine, women and song. I deny this categorically. Ninety percent of my interests were women.

Arthur Rubinstein

She's descended from a long line her mother listened to.

Gypsy Rose Lee

There is no greater fan of the opposite sex than me, and I have the bills to prove it.

Alan Jay Lerner

Sexual intercourse is like having someone else blow your nose.

Philip Larkin

I discarded a whole book because the leading
character wasn't on my wave-length. She was a
lesbian with doubts about her masculinity.

Peter De Vries

Sex is the most fun I ever had without laughing.

Woody Allen

The big difference between sex for money and sex
for free is that sex for money usually costs a lot
less.

Brendan Behan

The main problem with honest women is not how
to seduce them, but how to take them to a private
place. Their virtue hinges on half-open doors.

Jean Giraudoux

Have you ever been suddenly confronted with an
earring in your bed and come up with a perfectly
logical explanation?

Peter Pook

I'll come no more behind your scenes, David; for the silk stockings and white bosoms of your actresses excite my amorous propensities.

Samuel Johnson, to David Garrick

The average male thinks about sex every eleven minutes while he's awake.

Dr. Patrick Greene

My wife doesn't. Understand me?

William Cole

The censors wouldn't even let me sit on a guy's lap, and I've been on more laps than a table-napkin.

Mae West

An orgy looks particularly alluring seen through the mists of righteous indignation.

Malcolm Muggeridge

There are two good reasons why men go to see her. Those are enough.

Howard Hughes, on Jane Russell

"I've spent enough on you to buy a battleship," the Prince of Wales (later Edward VII) complained to his mistress, Lillie Langtry.

She replied, "And you've spent enough in me to float one."

Sexism

Why did I call this chapter 'Leave It to Beaver'? Because that's what some of the men at NBC News called *Overnight*, the first network news program run by women.

Linda Ellerbee

Shakespeare

A bishop sat through a complete performance of "A Midsummer Night's Dream" played entirely by schoolgirls. Praising their performance in a speech of thanks he said, "I think this is the first time I have ever seen a female Bottom."

Cyril Fletcher

An intense French actor, beginning Hamlet's speech to Gertrude with "mère, mère," sounds exactly like a sheep.

Paul Jennings

Hamlet's experience simply could not have happened to a plumber.

George Bernard Shaw

George Bernard Shaw

George Bernard Shaw is the first man to have cut a swathe through the theatre and left it strewn with virgins.

Frank Harris

Signs

"All vegetables in this establishment have been washed in water especially passed by the management."

Sign on tables, hotel in Sri Lanka

Sin/Sinning

Christ died for our sins. Dare we make his martyr-
dom meaningless by not committing them?

Jules Feiffer

There are three sorts of sin: little sins, bigger
ones, *and taking off your shoes without undoing
the laces.*

British nanny, quoted by Jonathan Gathorne-Hardy

The manufacture of sin is so easy a manufacture,
that I am convinced man could readily be per-
suaded that it was wicked to use the left leg as
much as the right; whole congregations would
only permit themselves to hop.

Sir Arthur Helps

The wages of sin is death and, in times like these,
it is the only decent salary we can get.

Louis Phillips

🐛

Singing

She was a singer who had to take any note above
A with her eyebrows.

Montague Glass

I can't sing. As a singist I am not a success. I am
saddest when I sing. So are those who hear me.
They are sadder even than I am.

Artemus Ward

She was a town-and-country soprano of the kind
often used for augmenting grief at a funeral.

George Ade

Sleep

The amount of sleep required by the average person is about five minutes more.

Wilson Mizener

Sleep is death without the responsibility.
Fran Lebowitz

Harris went to sleep at once. I hate a man who goes to sleep at once. There is a sort of indefinable something about it which is not exactly an insult and yet is an insolence.
Mark Twain

Smoking

Smoking is one of the leading causes of statistics.
Fletcher Knebel

More than one cigar at a time is excessive smoking.

Mark Twain

Snobs

The French are tremendous snobs, despite that
rather showy and ostentatious Revolution.

Arthur Marshall

A certain amount of judicious snobbery is quite a
good thing, besides being amusing.

A. L. Rowse

Society

The parties remind me of the Gay Nineties—the
men are gay and the women are in their nineties.

Alice-Leone Moats, on Philadelphia society

Song Title

I Feel so Miserable Without You, It's Almost Like Having You Here.

Stephen Bishop

—⚓—

Speech

He had that spooky bass voice meant to announce that he had entered the kingdom of manhood, but Rosalie knew that he was still outside the gates.

John Cheever

Through the windows, I could hear the changing of the guard. The commands of the officers, shouting to their men, sounded like someone retching.

Cecil Beaton, at Buckingham Palace

You can't be happy with a woman who pronounces both *d's* in Wednesday.

Peter DeVries

211

He was a practiced orator and could make a very small amount of information go a long way.

George A. Birmingham

She talked in such an exaggerated, dated drawl that it was like pulling a Mars bar apart, the syllables stretching out in long glucose strands.

Kieth Waterhouse

Spelling

They spell it Vinci and pronounce it Vinchy; foreigners always spell better than they pronounce.

Mark Twain

English spelling would seem to have been designed chiefly as a disguise for pronunciation. It is a clever idea, calculated to check presumption on the part of the foreigner.

Jerome K. Jerome

English spelling is unusual because our language is a rich verbal tapestry woven together from the tongues of the Greeks, the Latins, the Angles, the Klaxtons, the Celtics, the 76'ers, and many other ancient peoples, all of whom had drinking problems.

Dave Barry

Spring

When Spring comes around, I merely write my tailor, send him a small sample of dandruff, and tell him to match it exactly.

Oliver Hereford

Statistics

Statistics are like a bikini. What they reveal is suggestive, but what they conceal is vital.

Aaron Levenstein

Storytelling

Religion, aristocracy, sex and mystery . . . Christ, said the Duchess, I'm pregnant. Whodunnit?

Somerset Maugham

Stupidity

He had been kicked in the head when young and believed everything he read in the Sunday papers.

George Ade

Suburbia

Some of the finest axe murders of our history have
been committed in the small community. Usually
the newspapers blame sex or incompatibility or
money, but this is absurd. Once one gets into the
routine of ' We must have the Andersons over
Thurday night,' and 'Saturday we're going to the
Yardley's!' and 'Sunday I've invited the Bechoffs
over because we've owed them for so long!' there's
nothing left but the axe.

Irving H. Tressler

A suburban mother's role is to deliver children
obstetrically once, and by car forever ever.

Peter DeVries

Success

All you need in this life is ignorance and confidence; then success is sure.

Mark Twain

Sunburn

Sunburn is very becoming—but only when it's even—one must be very careful not to look like a mixed grill.

Noel Coward

Superstitions

He's very superstitious—he thinks it's unlucky to walk under a black cat.

Max Kauffmann

Surprise

While it is undeniably true that people love a surprise, it is equally true that they are seldom pleased to suddenly and without warning happen upon a series of prunes in what they took to be a normal loin of pork.

Fran Lebowitz

Switzerland/The Swiss

They say that if the Swiss had designed these mountains they'd be rather flatter.

Paul Theroux, (English traveller referring to Alps)
Dalton Trumbo

The only nation I've been tempted to feel really racist about are the Swiss—a whole country of phobic handwashers living in a giant Barclays Bank.

Jonathan Raban

The only interesting thing that can happen in a Swiss bedroom is suffocation by a feather mattress.

6

Taxes

The thing generally raised on city land is taxes.

Charles Dudley Warner

☞

Teenagers

The only thing I ever said to my parents when I was a teenager was "hang up, I got it."

Carol Leifer

Remember that as a teenager you are at the last stage in your life when you will be happy to hear that the phone is for you.

Fran Lebowitz

Telegrams

STREETS FULL OF WATER STOP PLEASE
ADVISE

> *Robert Benchley, in a telegram sent to Vanity Fair*
> *magazine after his arrival in Venice, Italy.*

ANY TIDINGS OF LINDBERGH STOP LEFT
HERE WEEK AGO STOP AM WORRIED

> *Robert Benchley, to Charles Brackett*

Telephone

The telephone is a good way to talk to people
without having to offer them a drink.

> *Fran Leibowitz*

Television

The people I see on talk shows make me wonder about the education in this country and the dental care.

Nicky Silver

For years "The Danny Thomas Show" was doing the ten commandments. Every episode had a little message to deliver: Don't lie, don't kill your neighbor, don't covet your neighbor's wife, don't uncover your neighbor's wife . . .

Mel Brooks

Whoever said that you can't get a quart in a pint pot has never watched a TV commercial.

Louis Phillips

Temptation

Lead me not into temptation. I can find the way myself.

Rita Mae Brown

I can resist everything except temptation.
Oscar Wilde

You oughtn't to yield to temptation.

Well, somebody must, or the thing becomes absurd.
Sir Anthony Hope Hawkins

Ten Commandments

Moses probably said to himself, "Must stop now or I shall be getting silly." That is why there are only ten commandments.
Mrs. Patrick Campbell

American girl on Commandments: "They don't tell you what you ought to do; and they only put ideas into your head."
Elizabeth Bibesco

Candidates should attempt no more than six of these.

*Anonymous, suggested addendum to the
Ten Commandments*

Texas

You know it takes forever to get out of Texas. And then when you do, you're in Oklahoma.

David Ball, country and western singer

Theater

I am quite prepared to admit that during my fifty-odd years of theatre-going I have on many occasions been profoundly moved by plays about the common man, as in my fifty-odd years I have frequently enjoyed tripe and onions.

Noel Coward

In the old days, ptomaine poisoning was a cover-all. If you missed a show and you were young, it meant you were having an abortion. If you were old, it meant you were having a face lift.

Ruth Gordon

. . . an evening spent at a Pinter play, nearly the whole of which she had sat wondering what in God's name had happened to the prompter.

Peter De Vries

Nobody can possibly have any adequate conception of what occurred during the creation week described in Genesis unless he has seen a musical revue in the making.

Heywood Broun

The great ham actor, Sir Donald Wolfit, announced from the stage, "Next week, we shall be performing *Hamlet*. I myself will take the part of the Dane, and my dear wife will play Ophelia." "Booo!" came a voice from the gods. "That old rat-bag!" "Nevertheless," Wolfit replied. "She will still be playing Ophelia."

Sir Donald Wolfit

"What's *Rosencrantz and Guildenstern* about?" One woman on opening night came up to Tom Stoppard and said, "What is your play about?" And he said, "It's about to make me very rich."

Gary Oldman

Dramaturgy always sounded to me like a nasty intestinal complaint.

Sheridan Morley

Jerome Kern was having trouble with an actress in *Show Boat*. She had an irritating habit of rolling her r's. "You want me to c-r-r-ross the stage," she said. "How am I supposed to get ac-r-r-r-oss the stage?" "Why don't you just roll on your r's?" suggested Kern.

Jerome Kern

The actor who took the role of King Lear played the king as though he expected someone to play the ace.

Eugene Field

I find writing about the Canadian theater or drama depressingly like discussing the art of dinghy-sailing among beduoins.

Merrill Denison

Thinking

An Englishman thinks seated; a Frenchman, standing; an American, pacing; an Irishman, afterward.

Austin O'Malley

Threats

You may be too old to spank, but I've still got my staple gun.

Robert Urich to Faye Dunaway in "It Had to Be You"

Threes

"Fire, Water, Woman, are Man's ruin!" Says wise Professor Van der Bruin.

Matthew Prior

Three difficult things: climbing a wall that's leaning toward you, kissing a girl who's leaning away, and making a speech at a cocktail party.

Anonymous

The three coldest things in the world: a blacksmith's anvil, a dog's nose, a woman's bottom.

Gaelic proverb

There are three roads to ruin: women, gambling, and technicians. The most pleasant is with women, the quickest is with gambling, but the surest is with technicians.

Georges Pompidou

Time

Daylight-saving time blossoms once more and is welcomed heartily by insomniacs who now have less night to be up all of.

Fran Lebowitz

Nothing troubles me more than time and space; and yet nothing troubles me less, as I never think about them.

Charles Lamb

If time were the wicked sheriff in a horse opera, I'd pay for riding lessons and take his gun away.

W.H. Auden

Titles

The Ancient Mariner would not have taken so well if it had been called The Old Sailor.

Samuel Butler

If *Hamlet* had been written in three days, it probably would have been called *The Strange Affair at Elsinore*.

J. M. Barrie

Toast

Hot buttered toast is surely what one would dream of on a desert island, rather than caviar and Krug. After serving on a windjammer on one of the last of those three-month sailing voyages to Australia, Eric Newby found he wanted to nothing so much as toast, which he pursued and devoured in prodigious quantity.

John Bayley

Trains

Sir,
Saturday morning, although recurring at regular and well-for-seen intervals, always seems to take this railway by surprise.

W. S. Gilbert, complaining by letter to the station-master of the Metropolitan Line at Baker Street

Translation

A translation, like a wife, is seldom strictly faithful
if it is in the least attractive.

Anonymous

Travel

There are two classes of travel—first class, and
with children.

Robert Benchley

The actual physical discomfort of traveling with
the kiddies is not so great, though you do emerge
from it looking as if you had just moved the piano
upstairs, single-handed.

Robert Benchley

If God meant us to travel tourist class he would
have made us narrower.

Martha Zimmerman

Abroad is unutterably bloody and foreigners are fiends.

Rose Macaulay

Twins

There are two things in this life for which we are never fully prepared and that is twins.

Josh Billings

Typewriters

When IBM invented the electronic typewriter everybody thought the company was made up of idiots because nobody had complained about the typewriter as it was.

Kurt Vonnegut

I know so little about the typewriter that once I bought a new one because I couldn't change the ribbon on the one I had.

Dorothy Parker

ॐ

Ugliness

Her features did not seem to know the value of teamwork.

George Ade

Mrs. Patrick Campbell, at a concert by famous coloratura. The artist came on. Mrs. Pat, taking one look at the singer's enormous jowl, stopped chatting to the dutchess at her side and said, "My God! She looks like I do in a spoon!"

James Agate

She looked like one of those potatoes that people photograph and send to the papers because it bears resemblance to a human face.

Monica Dickens

Miss ----- has a forehead like a Siamese kitten and a mouth like a galosh.

Mrs. Patrick Campbell

Understatement

Speaking of understatement, one reader has sent in the reminder that there is a pretty good one in the 17th chapter of Matthew, 23d verse.

Alexander Woollcott

13th—I went out to Charing Cross, to see Major-General Harrison hanged, drawn, and quartered; which was done there, he looking as cheerful as any man could be in that condition.

Samuel Pepys

Undertakers

I have nothing against undertakers personally. It's just that I wouldn't want one to bury my sister.

Jessica Mitford

Vaudeville

One man smashed a milk bottle and lay down on the pieces while they put a heavy roller over him. Then they drove a Mercedes truck over him. Plainly this skill would come in handy any time you fell asleep on a broken milk bottle in the middle of an autobahn.

Clive James

Vegetarian

A vegetarian is a person who won't eat anything that can have children.

David Brenner

I'm not a vegetarian because I love animals; I'm a vegetarian because I hate plants.

A. Whitney Brown

Vice-Presidents

On ships they call them barnacles; in radio they attach themselves to desks, and are called vice-presidents.

Fred Allen

The Vice-Presidency of the United States isn't worth a pitcher of warm spit.

Vice President John Nance Garner

Wales/The Welsh

There are still parts of Wales where the only concession to gaiety is a striped shroud.

Gwyn Thomas

Wall Street

"Wall Street," reads the sinister old gag, "is a street with a river at one end and a graveyard at the other." This is striking, but incomplete. It omits the kindergarten in the middle.

Frederick Schwed, Jr.

I recall that one of the first investment bankers I met taught me a poem.

God gave you eyes,
plagiarize.

A handy ditty when competing with other firms.

Michael Lewis

War

I read in newspapers that a German army had invaded France and was fighting the French, and that the English expeditionary force had crossed the Channel. "This,—I said to myself—'means war'". As usual I was right.

Stephen Leacock

I have never understood this liking for war. It panders to instincts already catered for within the scope of any respectable domestic establishment.

Alan Bennett

I have already given two cousins to the war and stand ready to sacrifice my wife's brother.

Artemus Ward

British officer on leave during World War I, describing what it was like to be in battle, "Oh, my dear fellow, the noise, the confusion . . . and the *people!*"

Washington, D.C.

Washington is Salem. If we're not lynching somebody twenty-four hours a day in this wretched town, we're not happy.

Tom Korologos, Washington lobbyist

Wasting Time

One favorite way of wasting time is trying to say something in praise of paper towels.

Franklin Pierce Adams

Weather

I said, "It's most extraordinary weather for this time of year." He replied, "Ah, it ain't this time of year at all."

Oliver St. John Gogarty

I'm leaving because the weather is too good. I hate London when it's not raining.

Groucho Marx

Witticisms

Are you going to come quietly or do I have to use ear-plugs?

Spike Milligan

Either he's dead or my watch has stopped.

Groucho Marx, feeling a pulse

One day I shot an elephant in my pyjamas. How it got into my pyjamas I'll never know.

Groucho Marx

Alexander Woollcott

A butterfly in heat.

Louis Untermeyer

Women

"Wimmin's a toss-up," said Uncle Pentstemon. "Prize packets they are, and you can't tell what's in 'em till you took 'em home and undone 'em."

H. G. Wells

She takes herself asunder still when she goes to bed, into some twenty boxes; and about next day noon is put together again, like a great German clock.

Ben Jonson

Joan used to walk across a ballroom as though she was trudging through deep snow.

Noel Coward

Remember, Ginger Rogers did everything Fred Astaire did, but backwards and in high heels.

Faith Whittlesey

Why haven't women got labels on their foreheads saying "Danger: Government Health Warning: Women can seriously damage your brains, genitals, current account, confidence, razor blades, and good standing among your friends."

Jeffrey Bernard

American women expect to find in their husbands a perfection that English women only hope to find in their butlers.

Somerset Maugham

That gentlemen prefer blondes is due to the fact that apparently, pale hair, delicate skin and an infantile expression represent the very apex of a frailty which every man longs to violate.

Alexander King

A woman without a man is like a fish without a bicycle.

Gloria Steinem

He always felt that one day she would pick him up, shove him in her handbag, and click the fastening to.

Malcolm Bradbury

Women really go beyond the call of duty to attract men. I wonder what a man would do in a similar situation. Let's say someone decided that in order for a man to look attractive in a bathing suit to a woman he had to pour hot wax dangerously near to the most sensitive part of his body and have it ripped off at least once every two months. How many men do you think would sign up? I think Evil Knievel would say, 'Too risky.'

Rita Rudner

She was a lovely girl. Our courtship was fast and furious—I was fast and she was furious.

Max Kauffmann

When a woman tells you her age, it's alright to look surprised, but don't scowl.

Wilson Mizener

She's the sort of woman who lives for others—you can always tell the others by their hunted expression.

C. S. Lewis, *The Screwtape Letters*

Word Play

"One night I asked my nurse if she could think of a seven-letter word in which the letter U appears three times. She sighed and said, "It's probably unusual." I told her that it was and it wasn't, and she slipped out of the room.

James Thurber

Words

You won't play that tape on your station—every other word begins with an "f" and ends with a "k." And it ain't firetruck.

Pete Rose, radio interview

There is one word in America that says it all, and that one word is, "You'll never know."

Joaquin Andujar, pitcher for the Houston Astros

I like words of one syllable and it works out very well in the French order for general mobilisation. The printed thing gives all the detail and then it says the *army de terre, de mer et de l'air.* That is very impressive when you read it in every village.

Gertrude Stein

I can answer you in two words—impossible.

Samuel Goldwyn

At the words "marry again" Mr. Llewellyn shuddered strongly like a blancmange in a high wind.

P.G. Wodehouse

Work

Anyone can do any amount of work, provided it isn't the work he is supposed to be doing.

Robert Benchley

I like work: it fascinates me, I can sit and look at it for hours. I love to keep it by me; the idea of getting rid of it nearly breaks my heart.

Jerome K. Jerome

Writing

I use the Palmer method, and a pad on a music stand. I'm not interested in computers, though they're less complex than the human brain—which I also try to use.

Saul Bellow

The shelf life of the modern hardback writer is somewhere between the milk and the yoghurt.

Calvin Trillin

I wrote a short story because I wanted to see
something of mine in print other than my fingers.

Wilson Mizener

Most writers I give fifty pages to get the shit
moving.

Terry McMillan

A free-lance writer is a man who is paid per piece
or per word or perhaps.

Robert Benchley

Writing is turning your worse moments into
money.

J. P. Donleavy

When I am asked what kind of writing is the most
lucrative, I have to say, ransom notes.

H. N. Swanson, literary agent

A new regulation for the publishing industry: "The
advance for a book must be larger than the check
for the lunch at which it was discussed."

Calvin Trillin

Writers are like seducers. They require three things: appetite, craft and self-confidence. Only the last two can be taught.

Clive Sinclair

In the Soviet Union a writer who is critical, as we know, is taken to a lunatic asylum. In the United States, he's taken to a talk show.

Carlos Fuentes

Everybody sooner or later turns out to be a writer. Get deep enough into anybody's confidence, and you find that he has manuscript. Psychoanalysts build a false science on the theory that millions of people are maladjusted lovers; a better knowledge of the world would teach that they are maladjusted writers.

Alva Johnston

After being turned down by numerous publishers, he decided to write for posterity.

George Ade

Youth

The young always have the same problem—how
to rebel and conform at the same time. They have
now solved this by defying their parents and copy-
ing one another.

Quentin Crisp, The Naked Civil Servant